OUT OF
THE MAZE

A COVENANTAL VIEW OF HOPE

OUT OF THE MAZE

DR. JIM HALLA

AMBASSADOR INTERNATIONAL
GREENVILLE, SOUTH CAROLINA & BELFAST, NORTHERN IRELAND

www.ambassador-international.com

Out of the Maze

A Covenantal View of Hope

© 2022 by Dr. Jim Halla

ISBN: 978-1-64960-115-5

eISBN: 978-1-64960-165-0

Cover Design by Hannah Linder Designs
Interior Typesetting by Dentelle Design

AMBASSADOR INTERNATIONAL
411 University Ridge Suite B14
Greenville, SC 29609, USA
www.ambassador-international.com

AMBASSADOR BOOKS
The Mount
2 Woodstock Link
Belfast, BT6 8DD, Northern Ireland, UK
www.ambassador-international.com

The colophon is a trademark of Ambassador

Contents

Introduction

THE WORD *HOPE* HAS TAKEN on a new dimension in the wake of the Coronavirus (COVID-19) pandemic. Prior, the idea of hope was already tarnished. Previously, America was faced with war on terrorism, the bombing of the Twin Towers, global unrest, and increasing uncertainty in the United States. Now Americans are experiencing times to which they had previously considered themselves immune. With the ongoing pandemic, God has increased the pressure on individuals and the Church to define and implement hope His way, for His glory and the good of His people.

The present-day mindset is an extension of the atmosphere developed in the wake of two world wars. The pandemic has highlighted the importance of defining hope God's way. World-wide circumstances are associated with a myriad of responses and counsel. People are "on the run," so to speak. Endless uncertainty, doubt, worry, and fear are the prevailing mindsets and the plight for many Americans. Many pundits have stepped in and given their analysis, even emphasizing the victimhood of humanity. We are also told to be "cool" because stress is bad for you. In that case, you are your hope.

The implications are that we once had hope, but now people are not so sure. Hope is closely associated with "world events" but *especially* when they affect us personally. We read in newspapers or hear on television various questions from a variety of venues that can best be summarized as: What is your hope?

Since you are reading this, you are probably interested in this topic, either for yourself or someone you know. I am sure you have heard many answers to the question "What is your hope?" You will surely continue to hear answers from many sources in the days and years ahead. In this book, you will hear another that is, in fact, not new at all. Before reading further, please do a brief and initial "hope" self-inventory by answering the following questions:

1. What is your hope for your present life, including the present circumstances and the life to come?
2. What is the source of that hope?
3. What influence does your hope have on your thinking and behavior?

The purpose of this self-inventory is to place you in a position to compare your answers with the information that follows. This book is designed to help you discover that there is true hope, and that this hope doesn't depend on circumstances or people. So, let's get started.

CHAPTER 1

Hope So, Maybe

"HOPE" IS A WORD THAT you hear regularly. When hope is defined using non-Biblical sources, it lacks a proper vertical reference. Thus, it is a false hope. Let's consider several of those sources.

According to *Webster's Dictionary*, "hope" may be a noun or verb. The dictionary tells us that hope is "a feeling of wanting that something will happen, a desire accompanied by expectation, and the thing one has a hope for or in." There is a *subjective* aspect of hope.

Practically, people may say: "I hope it doesn't rain." Or you might hear it another way: "We sure need rain. I hope it does rain and soon." Children may say: "I hope we get there soon." Adults may say something like this: "I hope he doesn't keep acting like that. I don't like it." People even talk about future longings—they dream of having or being something. In my medical office, I hear hope expressed this way: "I hope you can help me get relief," or "I hope you have something to get rid of or control this pain," or "My hope is that you cure me."

These statements from daily life express common features of hope. Hope is *fundamental* to life and influences every aspect of it. The desire for hope is *common,* even *universal,* among all types of people. It has no age or gender barriers.

Another common feature is *expectation,* which is often used as a synonym for hope. A person looks ahead waiting for something to happen or not to happen. Sometimes, this expectation is expressed as a dream or a wish and may be termed daydreaming, or fantasizing, or simply using one's imagination. Sometimes hope is a want or even a demand. The expectation, dream, wish, want, or demand *motivates* a person to spend his time thinking, desiring, and acting in certain ways. A person may spend increasing amounts of time thinking, planning, or even scheming how to fulfill his expectations.

There is a *cognitive* aspect of hope. Every person is a *hoper* who has identified himself as having expectations and at least one hope. In anticipation of having his hope realized, he sets and pursues an agenda for that hope to be realized. Much effort is exerted in terms of thinking, wanting, and acting as he hopes that his hope will be fulfilled. What he sets his hope upon occupies his whole person, including his thinking and wanting, which controls his actions. Similarly, what occupies his thoughts and desires is where he sets his hope. There is a reason or basis for a person's hope. Most often, it is based on what a person expects to get (or not get) from another person, event, or circumstance.

To instill hope in a patient, a medical doctor or related medical professional may speak of improved health, of maintaining good health, of a cure, or of relief; whatever seems most practical. However, because we live in a fallen world, having a body that won't wear out or hurt is not possible. Therefore, a person's hope may be only a "hope so"—an uncertainty or an expectation that may not be fulfilled. The issue for the person is not only his hope but also his standard for hope. In addition, an important aspect of hope is the person's efforts to attain hope and his response if his hope is not realized to his satisfaction.

The contemporary wisdom of the age places a high premium on hope. In fact, targeting hope is a major instrument in selling almost anything. McDonalds encourages people to buy burgers based on the idea that "you deserve a break today." McDonalds knows that people expect certain things in life—*break* and *that hope*. The United States Armed Services tried to entice recruits by the slogan: *Be all you can be in the Army*. What is it that you can be? Whatever it is, it is something that *hopefully* drives a person and influences him to think and enlist. Similarly, those who advertise homes or vehicles present the object to be sold as *your dream home* or *your vehicle*. People have anticipations and *hoped-for* expectations.

The key descriptive word for these kinds of hope is *hope so*. False hope is characterized by a *lack of certainty*. It may be defined as *an uncertain anticipation or expectation*. The thing *hoped for* may or may not occur. One can't be sure either way.

Yet, in one sense, there is no such thing as a hopeless person. "How so?" you ask, since so many people are described with such terminology. Everyone has either hope or some sort of *hope so*. In the so-called hopeless person, his expectation may have shrunk or might be non-existent. His hope has not come true; what he had hoped for he didn't get. Or what he hoped for and in has not produced the results he desired. The problem is not hope but the source and object of one's hope and the motivation to get it. More will be said later about the hopeless person.

Truly, everyone is a *hoper*—one who hopes. Moreover, since everyone has hope, or better, everyone has some sort of hope, hope then is something that you *possess* as well as *do*.

Before reading further, please answer these questions:

Application

1. How do you define hope? How do others and the dictionary define it?
2. What are some characteristics and themes of hope?
3. Where did it come from and how did you get it?
4. What is your basis or standard hope?
5. How does your definition of hope affect your thoughts, desires, and actions and vice versa?
6. What is a major underlying theme for those who hope?

CHAPTER 2
A Perplexing Situation

UP TO THIS POINT, I have used several sources in order to define and demonstrate hope, including the experiences from daily life, *Webster's Dictionary*, the doctor's office, and the contemporary wisdom of the culture. A working definition for hope derived from these sources would be something like this: *hope is an attitude of expectation of possible fulfillment for right now or present-day living that is an uncertain hope-so*. Moreover, everybody has hope or at least some type of expectation. Hope motivates him such that he has placed his trust and focus in and on it. He looks forward to having it happen or not happen. At the same time, we learned that everybody needs hope.

The last section highlighted a perplexing situation. We are faced with the reality that everybody needs hope and clings to some type of hope. People have something that they hope for and expect to happen. That hope may change depending on changes in the person and what is happening in his life. For instance, someone with good health may hope to continue in it. However, if he develops a disease, his hope will likely change. He is not interested or hopeful of good health. Rather his focus and hope are getting relief and or a cure. The problem may be a physical one or it may simply be what people call a *life* problem. A person may be desirous of something happening or not happening in his life. We must be careful how we use words. *Life* is God's providence—His power and authority. *Life* does not have a *life* of its own. *Life* never just is!

If hope is universal (everybody has some type of hope), and it is necessary for life (everybody needs it), how is it that so many people fail to respond in a God-honoring way to difficulties, people, and situations that a providential God brings into their lives? Some may disagree with that sentence. They would not want their responses to be considered in terms of non-God-honoring thoughts, desires, and actions. They would not want their responses to be scrutinized under the microscope of Scripture. Too often people, including believers, function as if circumstances control their responses and offer an excuse for any response such as "I am under a lot of stress." However, they are responsible for their responses and their responses reflect their views of God, themselves, and their circumstances.

There are several possibilities to explain the perplexing situation presented in these first two sections. I have chosen three factors to help us better define the hopeless person and move us toward a definition of true hope. They are the person's definition of hope, the person hoping (hope is a verb), the source of the hope (verb is a noun), or a combination of all three.

In order to find God's answer to this seemingly perplexing situation, we must turn to the only reliable authority for life and Godliness: God's Word (Isaiah 8:20; Ezra 7:10; 2 Peter 1:3-4).[1] It is a non-negotiable fact that believers must consult God's Word for all aspects of life. I will follow the Bible's example of "discrimination by separation" (which is known as discernment and wisdom) in order to compare true and false hope.

The Bible teaches that life is divided into two antithetical ways of living. The Bible presents this teaching using a variety of terms: saved and unsaved, narrow and wide roads, lost and found, clean and unclean, and light and darkness. So, too, the Bible presents and explains hope as true hope and false hope. These two are diametrically opposed. Moreover, false hope is no hope at all.

God designed man as an inside-out person. Man is told to guard his heart because it is the wellspring of life (Proverbs 4:23). Man is motivated by what reigns in his heart: what he thinks,

---

1   Isaiah 8:20: *To the law and to the testimony! If they do not speak according to this word, they have no light of dawn.* Ezra 7:10: *For Ezra had devoted himself to the study and observance of the Law of the Lord, and to teaching its decrees and laws in Israel*—see Nehemiah 8:3-8; 2 Peter 1:3-4: *Since His divine power has given us everything for life and godliness through the full knowledge of the One Who called us by His own glory and might (through which He has given to us valuable, indeed, the greatest promise of all, in order that through these you might become partakers of a divine nature, having escaped from the corruption that is in the world because of desire.*

desires, and hopes. A person's thoughts and desires express the treasures of his heart (Matthew 6:24-34; 15:1-20; Mark 7:1-23).

People live out of their heart and their hope and they live for that hope. Hope and what a person treasures are interrelated. Thus, hope is a motivating force in one's life. And yet, hope may change depending on what is happening around him or her. For instance, someone with good health may hope to continue in that condition. However, if he develops a disease, his hope and focus will likely change. He will not be as interested or hopeful of a cure or good health but of getting relief.

Application

1. What standards are available to define hope? What is yours and why?
2. What is the dilemma referred to in this section regarding hope?
3. What are some terms that the Bible uses to describe an antithetical mindset and way of life?
4. Write out your definition of true and false hope.

CHAPTER 3

Man is a Hopeful Being by God's Creational Design

You may be thinking: What happened to man so that he finds himself a hopeful being—one who has a hope and seeks after it—and yet is so often disappointed? Only God's Word gives us the correct answer. There are many counterfeit answers but only God, in His sufficient, authoritative, and infallible Word can be trusted. Very simply, God created man, the image of God, a hopeful creature. Therefore, hope is an essential part of human life.

How is this so? Adam, before the fall, and Jesus Christ, while on earth, both had hope and expectations. These two people showed us what normal is. They set the standard for what God intended for and in His people. Consider Adam. In the perfect world of the Garden prior to the fall, Adam had expectations. What were they? The Bible doesn't tell us completely, but Adam was able to look forward to all that the tree of life held out (Genesis 2:9, 15-17). At least, this included the giving and sustaining of life by God Himself and the promise of immortality. Otherwise, God's warning of the punishment of death would have been an empty one.

Adam expected eternal life in God's presence. This hope conditioned all that he did prior to the fall. His hope was a present reality that affected how he lived. Apparently, he looked forward to that which was promised but had not yet been fulfilled. What had not come—but was promised by God— so influenced Adam that he thought of it as already having been accomplished. The fulfillment of what God promised affected Adam's daily thoughts, desires, and actions such that he was able to function as a God-pleaser.

Adam's situation is a prelude to what people term the *already* and *not yet*. Adam had fellowship with God (the *already* or even *the now*) but it was not Adam's final destiny (the *not yet*). Pre-fall, Adam saw, tasted, touched, heard, and smelled (he had a sensual sensory experience) when he was in the Garden. Initially, he knew he was God's man: a dependent creature in perfect fellowship with the Creator and Controller. He was living in the *now* and *already* apparently in sync with God. His hope was the fulfillment of what he had. How much he looked ahead and desired more of what he had we are not told.

Next, consider Jesus Christ, the perfect man in an imperfect world. He knew what hope was all about. His life on earth was influenced and directed by the anticipation of what God had in store for Him (Hebrews 12:1-3).[2] He looked forward

2   Hebrews 12:1-3: *Therefore since we are surrounded by such a great cloud of witnesses, we must put off every weight and the sin that is so readily found*

to pleasing His Father, which included a proper response to His humiliation. Pleasing His Father and accomplishing His Father's goal enabled Jesus to return to the Father and to the glory He had prior to His incarnation as Victor, Author, and Perfector of His people and their saving faith (John 4:31-34; 17:1,5,24-26; Hebrews 12:1-3).[3]

How about believers? God chose them to be in relationship to Jesus Christ before the foundation of the world (Ephesians 1:4). Therefore, based on the believer's relationship with Christ by the Holy Spirit, the believer has hope. The believer's hope is founded on Christ the Hope of Glory, His accomplished work, and His resurrection (Colossians 1:27). The Triune God poured His love into the hearts of believers through the indwelling Holy Spirit; as a result, love and hope does not disappoint (Romans 5:1-5).[4] Based on these truths, Paul taught that all things are to be

---

all around us, and we must run the race that has been set before us with perseverance, looking off to Jesus, the Author and Completer of our faith, Who for the joy that had been set before Him, endured the cross, despising its shame, and is seated at the right hand of God's throne. Consider Him Who endured such opposition from sinners against Himself, so that you won't get tired and give up.

3   John 4:31-34: *Meanwhile His disciples encouraged Him, "Rabbi, eat." But He said to them, "I have food to eat that you don't know anything about." So they said to one another, "Somebody hasn't brought Him something to eat, has he?" Jesus said to them, "My food is to do the will of the One Who sent me and to finish His work."*

4   Romans 5:1-5: *Therefore, having been declared righteous by faith we have peace with God through our Lord Jesus Christ. Through Whom also by faith we have been led into this grace in which we stand and we boast about the hope of God's glory. But not only that; indeed we also boast about afflictions knowing that affliction produces endurance and endurance approval and approval hope. We need not be ashamed of hope because God's love has been poured into our hearts through the Holy Spirit Who has given to us.*

used by the believer to produce Christlikeness, including true hope (Romans 8:28-29).[5]

Probably, you have seen evidence in your own life of the fact that man is a hopeful being. Consider the "hopeless" person mentioned previously. You may have experienced or witnessed this condition. What is hopelessness? A hopeless person's hope has not been met. Something else happened to him that he did not expect and/or he did not want. What he hoped in and for did not happen. It may be as simple as a child looking forward to an outdoor swimming party or ball game only for it to be rained out. Or it could be the hope of a body that works "like it did when I was twenty years old," only to receive a diagnosis of cancer or arthritis. The thing hoped for didn't occur.

We speak of these situations as "dashed hopes" or "coming up empty-handed." Clearly, the basis for the hopeless person's hope did not produce what he expected. He was disappointed because his hope failed him. His hope did not produce "the goods," so to speak. This is in stark contrast to God's truth as given in Romans 5:5: the believer is not to be ashamed of true hope because God and His hope never fails. Since the hopeless person is one whose hopes and expectations were not met,

---

5   Romans 8:28-29: *We know that God makes everything work together for the good of those who love Him, for those who are called according to His purpose, because those whom He foreknew, He also foreordained to be conformed to His image's so that He might the First-born among many brothers.*

if this is a regular occurrence, he may come to expect "failed expectations." The culture would call this person a pessimist or say he is "depressed" or "stressed." He acts on the belief that his expectations will never be met. He may be fearful to look forward, and therefore, he doesn't. He may become disappointed and discouraged, and eventually he may lose heart. He gives in and he gives up. "What's the use" or "It doesn't really matter" is often his attitude.

When you hear about someone's "dashed hopes," you should consider an element that is too often ignored. This element is the person's response when he doesn't get what he has hoped for. "Dashed hopes" are one thing; the person's response is another. His response to failed expectations very often depends on the object of his hope and how important the individual thought it to be. Although people respond differently, everyone responds when their hope is unfulfilled. Putting all this together, the issue is not hope or no hope. Rather, the issues are: *what is your hope, how do you intend to obtain it, and how do you respond if you don't get it?*

If it is true that every person is created a hopeful being (and it is), then we must define true hope. Before we do, it is important to remember our earlier definition of false hope: *it is an uncertain attitude of a hoped-for expectation and its possible fulfillment.* It involves thinking and wanting. Please remember that when sources other than the Bible are consulted, hope is at best a "hope so." Now we are ready to define true hope.

Application

1. What is God's creational design for man?
2. What is the significance of that design?
3. Describe *hopelessness* and *dashed hope*. What may be the problem?
4. What is the hopeless person's main consideration and focus?

CHAPTER 4

A Definition of True Hope: The *Already* and *Not Yet*

HAVING LOOKED AT SEVERAL CHARACTERISTICS of hope and determined that everybody has some type of hope, we now must define true hope. Two questions are fundamental in helping people obtain a clear perspective of hope. First, what is hope? Second, what standard do you use to determine its meaning? In order to answer the questions accurately, believers must consult God's Word (See footnote 1). Scripture is God's self-authenticating and self-attesting proclamation that God is Lord of lords and King of kings and that He takes care of His people for His glory and their good. Therefore, He deserves to be heard and followed. When we look at Scripture, we find that pre-fall Adam and Jesus Christ had hope, and that man is created a hopeful being. It follows that God has much to say about hope. How does the Bible define true hope and why does everybody need it?

The clearest place to find God's definition of hope is contained in Romans 8:24-25:

> For in this hope we were saved. But hope that is seen
> is no hope at all. Who hopes for what he already
> has? But if we hope for what we do not yet have,
> we wait for it patiently.

Paul writes that believers were saved with, and not by hope (as the King James Version incorrectly translates). True hope and its foundation are a gift imparted at salvation, but salvation is not delivered in one package. In a sense, believers are saved, are being saved, and will be saved. The hope of salvation begins with and includes the new birth (regeneration), the forgiveness of sin, being declared not guilty and accepted (justification), and being adopted into God's family. All of these are wonderful and hope-engendering and love-provoking in and of themselves. But it is true hope that buttresses saving faith and points one to Heaven. This motivates and sustains the believer to eagerly engage in "life after salvation"—to grow in Christlikeness in thought, desire, and action—while on earth (Colossians 3:1-3; 1 John 3:1-3). In that way, they are preparing for Heaven.

In Romans 8:24-25, Paul stresses the necessity of salvation and true hope. Hope for the believer is to take hold of and make use of the expectation of these future blessings that begin at salvation. In other words, the Christian has been saved. That is a present reality which combines the *now* and the *already*. The believer is saved and is being saved as he lives as one saved; that is part of the *already*. There is joy living in the *now* as a new creature in Christ. Circumstances don't change that hope and should not change confidence in that hope.

The believer is looking forward to and preparing for Heaven on this earth. This is also part of the *already*. But the Christian knows that he will be saved eventually. This is part of the *not yet*: being in Heaven in the presence of God. The believer looks forward to the *not yet* while living in the *already* and *now* as if living eternally in the presence of the Triune God (the *not yet*) is a completed reality. In one sense it is (John 17:3; Romans 6:9-10). This type of forward gaze and expectation characterized Jesus as Messiah. It enabled Him to live, die, rise, and ascend as the Victor. It is to characterize the believer! The believer is to live as a saved person (the *already*) who is looking forward to something (the *not yet*) even more amazingly wonderful than his initial salvation and all the benefits and blessings that are associated with it.

Hope is especially necessary for Godly living given today's world and its problems, but there is nothing new *under the sun* (Ecclesiastes 1:9, 14). What is true today was true for believers in earlier times. Paul, in verse 25, writes that hope produces patience and steadfastness, both of which are needed for Godly endurance (Hebrews 12:1-3. See my book: *Endurance: What It Is and How It Looks In the Believer's Life*). Paul was speaking to Christians just like you and me. Times were not easy; they were not the way those Christians would have liked them to be. Things are no different today. In today's fast-paced world, believers are surrounded by purported wisdom from all sides, wooing them to come, see, and taste their answers and counsel. It was easy then, as now, to be seduced and pursue that which seems and feels *good* and *right*. True hope, as does its partner, saving faith, enables you, the believer, to keep your heart (inner man) and your eyes (outer man—your whole person, inner and outer man) focused on who God is; what He has promised; His resources and provisions for Godly thoughts, desires, and actions; and the expectation that He is truly The Promise-Keeper. True hope is necessary for living as a God-pleaser.

As good as regeneration, forgiveness of sin, justification, and adoption are, they are only the beginning—part of the *already*; there is more to come! Romans 8:24-25, which defines true hope, is preceded by verses 19-23. These speak of the groaning of creation (v.22) and compare believers to a woman in labor (v.23). The entire creation was affected by the fall and is subject to corruption, bondage, and futility. The meaning of the word translated as "groaning" includes sighing, as when someone is afflicted or burdened or in a tight spot (Romans 8:22-23; 2 Corinthians 5:2,-4; Hebrews 13:17). It is used in James 5:9 for grumbling and complaining and it is used in Mark 7:34 to describe Jesus as He looked up to Heaven and with a sigh called out to God. His prayer was heard. Moreover, Paul writes that the Holy Spirit groans (v.26-27).

A look into Romans 8:19-23 and the context of this portion of Scripture is in order to correctly interpret Paul's teaching in verses 24-25:

> The creation waits in eager expectation for the son of God to be revealed. For the creation was subjected to frustration, not by its own choice, but by the will of the one who subjected it, in hope the creation itself will be liberated from its bondage to decay and brought into the glorious freedom of the children of God. We know the whole creation has been groaning in the pains of childbirth right up to the present time. Not only so, but we ourselves who have the firstfruits of the Spirit groan inwardly as we wait eagerly for our adoption as sons, the redemption of our bodies.

Paul speaks of three groanings: the creation's, which begins at the fall and God's judgment (v.22; Genesis 3:15-17), the believer's, which begins at regeneration (v.23), and the Holy Spirit's in verses 26-27:

> In the same way, the Spirit helps us in our weakness. We do not know what we ought to pray for, but the Spirit himself intercedes for us with groans that words cannot express. And he who searches our

hearts knows the mind of the Spirit because the
Spirit intercedes for the saints in accordance with
God's will.

The groanings spoken of are not sinful because Jesus and
the Holy Spirit groaned (Mark 7:34). Moreover, groanings are
not complaints. Rather, they result from an honest assessment
and forward look at a future reality—the *not yet*.

In the context of a fallen world and failing bodies including
pandemics, it is proper for believers to eagerly anticipate and
look forward to future glory which had begun at their salvation.
True hope points creation and the believer beyond the *now/
already* toward the *not yet*. For creation, the *not yet* includes the
new heavens and the new earth (Matthew 19:28; Revelation 21-22).

For the believer there is the reality of a perfected regenerated
heart and sanctification which falls under the rubric of
glorification (Romans 8:29; 2 Corinthians 5:1-4; Colossians 3:1-
3; 1 John 3:1-3). In this way and from that mindset, the believer
is of earthly good! In fact, the believer groans because he is
rich—rich in the Spirit—and he is eagerly looking forward as
he moves toward even greater riches—the *not yet* (Romans
8:23-25). Paul characterized the groanings of the Holy Spirit as
His intercession for believers who don't know how to pray.
Christ intercedes for His people in Heaven and the Holy
Spirit intercedes for His people by dwelling in them and the

Church (Romans 8:34; Hebrews 7:25; Romans 8:9-11, 26-27). He strengthens believers in their weaknesses as they live in the *already* anticipating the *not yet*. This, too, is hope-engendering.

Let's return to Romans 8:19-22 in which Paul personifies creation. The response of creation is more than proper and it is a pattern for believers. Not only does creation sing praises to God, acknowledging and praising Him as the Creator, but here Paul writes that creation is conscious of the misery and burden of sin (Psalms 8 and 19). In that sense, creation imitates Christ (see Luke 13:1-5, 34-35; 19:41-44; 23:27-31; John 11:33-38). Christ did not groan without hope and neither does creation. Proper groaning has a forward, future perspective and honors God! Creation's sigh is an anticipatory sigh, as it awaits liberation and future redemption—the coming of new heavens and the new earth (v.20-21). Thus, creation focuses on God's promise (the *not yet*), not the present reality of living in a fallen world, including pandemics. Creation paid homage to the Triune God as Creator, Controller, Savior, and Redeemer. So, too, is the believer to do.

Mankind should learn from creation and Paul suggests that believers have. The Holy Spirt who lives within believers is the first fruits—the down payment—of the glory to be fully revealed (v.23)! Therefore, the believer's sigh should be an expression of an expectant, upward, eternal perspective based on knowledge; both the believer and creation eagerly await the final redemption (Romans 8:23-25). Their eyes are fixed on the finish line as Jesus was fixed not simply on completing the race but winning (Hebrews 12:1-3). This eternal perspective and proper vertical reference are critical for Godly endurance.

Paul focused believers living in the *now* and having experienced the *already* (salvation and its blessings) on the *not yet* which produced hope. True hope has its foundation in the Person of the Triune God and His provisions. True hope is based on God—His presence, His promises, His power to do what He has promised, and His provisions to become more like Christ in any and every situation.

True hope enables the believer to persevere and to run the race in *life* as a winner because Christ, the ultimate Winner, has gone before and is seated in the heavenlies (Hebrews 6:13-20; 12:1-3). In that sense, the believer lives in the *already* as a pilgrim, patiently and joyfully purifying himself as he looks forward to and prepares himself for his home in Heaven—the *not yet* (Philippians 3:21; Hebrews 6:18-20; 11:24-27; 1 John 3:1-3). Setting one's hope in and on the Triune God changes the focus from self to pleasing God, Who makes promises and keeps them for His glory and the believers' good. The believer has been a recipient of God's promise-making and promise-keeping, which is hope-engendering so he, too, runs the race as a victor because he is in Christ.

Circumstances, feelings, and reasoning divorced from the Bible will never trump the basis for true hope. Paul and Peter, as we will see later, taught the same message. Believers rightfully sigh due to the work of the indwelling Holy Spirit. The believer is not immune from hard times because of the possession of the Holy Spirit. Hard times will continue until Jesus returns.

Let's return to a closer look at verses 24-25 of Romans 8. Paul is speaking of bodily redemption, but he also speaks of sanctification—growing and changing—and ultimately, glorification. The destiny of all believers—being in the presence of the living God—produces true hope (or it should). Therefore, believers have and will live the resurrected life *now* (the *already*)! Paul is highlighting an aspect of the *already* and *not yet*. The believer is to be eagerly but patiently anticipating the *not yet* as they live in the *already*. The believer and the Church are in Christ indwelt by the Holy Spirit. Therefore, there is to be an eager anticipation of the present and future reality. This is to excite and to guide the believer while in the present life, as it did Jesus Christ.

Verse 25 of Romans 8 tells us that hope produces patience, endurance, and even steadfastness (also see Romans 5:1-5, footnote 4 and the discussion in Chapter 9). True hope along with saving faith give *spiritual eyes* to the believer (1 Corinthians 2:16; 2 Corinthians 5:7-9; 10:3-5). His interpretive grid has changed from a purely sensual experience based on his feelings, his reasoning divorced from biblical truth, and his experience—or all three. He looks past the *already/now* to the *not yet* and rejoices. In that he re-interprets the present through the eyes of a completed future!

When Paul wrote, he was speaking to Christians just like you and me. Times were very hard then, and things are no different for Christians today. There was no infectious pandemic, but Christians were constantly endangered. They were truly an endangered species at the hands of many Roman emperors—and even fellow Jews. In today's fast-paced world, surrounded by and bathed in a constant flow of purported wisdom, it is easy to try and go with the prevailing mindset. James speaks of this as doubting (1:5-8: see discussion of these verses in Chapter 9). This tossing about may be the result of accepting the "hopes" and expectations offered by today's culture. Some have postulated a hopeless world, its end being extinction and annihilation. Others simply reach for pleasure and fulfillment in the now. A proper eternal perspective does not influence how they live.

False hope is focused on *you* and *right now*. It does not have a proper focus on the *now* because it does not have a proper focus on the *already* or the *not yet*. Rather, true hope keeps your eyes and heart—your whole person—focused on God and the expectation that He is truly the Promise-maker and Promise-keeper. True hope brings the *already* and *not yet* in harmony.

A threefold and partial summary of Paul's teaching in Romans 8:19-22, 23-25 centers on the necessity of hope for the believer. First, he brings together the *already* and *not yet*. The believer takes hold of future blessings that begin at salvation and uses this reality to live as a God-pleaser now. The believer's expectation is no hope-so. It is the real thing! It is based on the work of the Triune God determined in eternity past. It is accomplished and guaranteed by Christ's finished work as Messiah, His continuing work as Priest, and the Spirit's presence in every believer and in His Church. The cross and Christ's resurrection is the Triune God's guarantee that hope is a gift and it is as true as He is! He does not give bad gifts or make false promises!

Second, I repeat that the hope Paul refers to in these passages is best summarized as the *already* and *not yet*. As good as the present blessings of salvation are (the *already*—the believer is saved and is being saved), there are still more wonderful things to come including Heaven (the *not yet*). The *not yet,* though, begins now! The believer will continue to grow into Christlikeness while on this earth. The future blessings of salvation include all that the tree of life and Adam looked forward to—an eternal inheritance and being in the presence of God. Moreover, in glory, every believer will have freedom from sin and bodily misery (Revelation 21:1-4).

Third, the believer has a relationship with the Triune God such that resurrection life begins *now* (Romans 6:9-11; 1 John 3:1-3). This is part of the *already*. The believer has been raised with Christ and is seated with Him in the heavenlies (Romans 6:9-11; 8:9-11; Colossians 3:1-3). The *already* is what we are in Christ by the Holy Spirit set apart for God, by God, and to God (Romans 11:33-36). As good as the present blessings of salvation are, there is still more to come. This is the *not yet*! Future blessings include all that the tree of life signified and Adam looked forward to. This includes eternal life and an eternal inheritance in the very presence of God. Not only that, but in glory every believer will have freedom from sin and bodily misery as described in Revelation 21-22. The believer's present and future hope is related to Christ's resurrection, ascension, and session as King of kings and Lord of lords (1 Timothy 1:17; 6:16-17). Proper theology gives rise to a right perspective now!

At this point in our study of hope based on Scripture, a definition of true hope is in order. *True hope is a real time, present reality manifested as a confident expectation and anticipation of the fulfillment of what God has promised*. Moreover, it is a *personal attitude of confident conviction and sure expectation of something good based on knowing that God makes promises, that*

He keeps those promises, and that every child of God is the recipient of those promises for God's glory and the good of the believer. This definition contrasts that of false hope that has been described will be discussed again in a later section.[6]

Let me be clear: good should be defined God's way. Good is best understood as the believer becoming more like Christ in any and every situation, which is God's providence (His control). In contrast to contemporary thought, the Bible stresses the certainty and clear-sighted perspective of true hope; it is never an uncertain "hope so." Hope's focus is always future-focused and eternal, which enables the believer to develop in Christlike thinking, wanting, and doing. In that way, the believer is of earthly good because of his proper heavenly focus. True hope keeps the person firmly planted on this earth until God calls him home—*to live is Christ*—and serving Him and His people now as His agent—*and to die is gain*—before being in His eternal presence as His child (Philippians 1:19-23).

In contrast to contemporary thought, the Bible stresses the certainty and clear-sighted perspective of true hope. It is never an *uncertain hope so*, because hope's foundation is what God has done in Christ. True hope focuses on the now—the believer's present life—but through the lens of eternal life and its blessings, which began at salvation. An eternal perspective

---

6   False hope is an attitude of expectation of possible fulfillment for the "now" that is an uncertain "hope so."

now enables the believer to keep moving toward the finish line as a winner. The dual focus—present and eternal—is based on the promises of God and their fulfillment. This dual focus enables the believer to run the race as Jesus did (Hebrews 12:1-3).

Jesus faced His own pandemic. It was not any virus. He came to His own but they rejected Him, the Sinless, Holy One because they loved darkness (John 1:5-9; 3:17-21). The pandemic was spiritual. Jesus stepped into misery and death but the people hated and rejected the true Light, Life and Hope and the Bringer of that hope. Jesus did not forsake His people. That is one reason why true hope is a reality and a necessity for living now in today's world with today's problems.

Application

1. Name the standard to be used and define true hope (see Romans 8:24-25).

2. What are the three groanings, who is doing them, and why? What is their significance?

3. Simply, what is the focus of true hope?

CHAPTER 5

Everyone Needs True Hope

HAVING DEFINED TRUE HOPE, LET'S discuss why everyone needs true hope. It is evident that everyone needs true hope, and that the only way anyone can have true hope is to be saved. We have learned that man was created a hope-based creature, that pre-fall Adam was a hopeful being, and that Jesus, to whom all believers are being conformed, had true hope—the confident expectation and even assurance that what had been ordained in eternity past would be accomplished in the Triune God's time and manner for His glory.

Did Christ have faith and hope? This is an interesting question. Some may quibble with or balk at the notion that Christ, the Godman, had hope and faith. He did not need saving faith and true hope. But the Spirit of God was on Him, preparing Him for the journey of His ministry (Isaiah 11:2).He trusted the Father as the Promise-maker and Keeper (John 6:37-43; 17:1-5, 24-26). As man, He learned: He increased in wisdom and stature and in favor before God and men (Luke 2:52) and He learned obedience (Hebrews 5:7). His faith and hope were intertwined with knowledge as God. But as man, He experienced all that man experienced but not as a sinner (Hebrews 4:14-16).

Christ had surety and conviction of who He was and His mission (John 4:31-34; Hebrews 12:1-3). He lived as if He had saving faith and true hope, but He was not a sinner in need of salvation. Inherently Jesus knew, trusted, and obeyed in order to accomplish the Triune God's plan of redemption and means of glory determined in eternity past. He looked forward, fully convinced and eagerly expecting that the Triune God would be fully satisfied (Hebrews 12:1-3).

Returning to the main theme, are there other factors that we should consider? Yes. After Adam sinned, man remained a hopeful creature, but true hope was lost. Before the fall, Adam had true hope because he was in a perfect world in a perfect relationship with God. God gave Adam marching orders, which he was to carry out as God's representative and co-regent (Genesis 1:28-30). Adam expected to carry out those marching orders, but once Adam sinned (and all mankind with him except Christ), every person continued to hope. However, the object, content, and motivation for and of hope was *false* and *misdirected*.

As a result of God's judgment, every person was considered guilty and condemned before God (Romans 3:23; 5:12-14; 6:23). Man lost his proper and original relationship with God and became His enemy. He became like his father Satan, developing a lifestyle of a God-hating self-pleaser (John 8:44; Ephesians 2:1-

3). Self took center stage; self-pleasing in lieu of God-pleasing became fallen man's modus operandi. Hope's focus began and ended with self. The underlying hope and expectation of life became "getting something for me." In a nutshell, every person (unless and until he is saved) has a false and misdirected hope. Although he lives in God's world, he denies that fact because he doesn't have Christ and Christ does not have him (Colossians 1:27; 1 Timothy 1:1).[7] Therefore, unbelievers need true hope.

There are many other consequences of Adam's first sin. One that is important to our discussion involves a person's thinking, wanting, hoping, and believing. All of these are heart or inner-man activities.[8] Since the fall, man's fundamental problem is his heart and that which flows from it. Fallen man has turned to self, sin, and Satan, and away from God. Therefore, man's thoughts, desires, motivations and ways are at cross purposes with God's (Isaiah 55:8-9; 1 Corinthians 2:14). As a result, what is said of man's misdirected and false hope can also be said about his faith and love. The triad of false hope, non-saving faith, and self-love (which is not biblical love at all but loyalty, allegiance, and devotion to self for self) are in opposition to God and stand

---

7   Colossians 1:27: *those to whom, God wished to make know what is the riches of the glory of this secret among the Gentiles, which is Christ in you, the hope of glory . . .* ; 1 Timothy 1:1: *Paul an apostle of Christ Jesus by order of God our Savior and of Christ Jesus our hope.*

8   The heart is used in Scripture to denote where man thinks, purposes, doubts, and fears that is known only to God perfectly and the person imperfectly. Man lives out of his heart: Matthew 12:34-37; 15:16-20; Mark 7:18-20; Luke 6:43-45; Proverbs 4:23.

in contrast to biblical hope, saving faith, and self-sacrificing love of God and neighbor.

Next, consider the believer. He also needs biblical hope. The Bible commands Christians to hope (Psalms 130:7; 131:3; 1 Peter 1:13; Hebrews 10:23). Interestingly and refreshingly, the Bible teaches that the God Who created man a hope-seeking being tells him to seek hope. Further, He promises he will find it because hope is a Person (Colossians 1:27). Hope is commanded and therefore it not an option. Hope is a *choice*, a matter of the will, but refreshingly and hope-engendering, one which the believer is equipped to make and act accordingly. Christians are accountable to God for their choice, which is hope-engendering because the believer knows that God does not make commands that He does not equip His people to keep. The issue is not hope or no hope but choosing the proper hope.

Peter commands true hope. First Peter 1:13 says, *Therefore, buckling the belts of your minds for action, keeping level-headed, set your hope entirely on the grace that will be brought to you at the revelation of Jesus Christ*.) As I have said, God doesn't give His people commands they are unable to keep. Moreover, if hope is commanded, hope must be of utmost importance to God. Further, if God has commanded hope and unbelievers don't have it, then God must provide it. If He provides it, true hope must be of utmost importance for His people.

In giving this command, Peter knew his congregation had no (or little) hope of avoiding and surviving upcoming persecutions, let alone maintaining physical well-being. Nero was soon to use the Christians for food for the lions and for human candles. Their situation was precarious, seemingly at Nero's bidding. Yet Peter told his people to set their hope entirely on God's grace, their salvation, and Christ's glorious return. Peter linked the *already* and not *yet*. Peter taught that hope was a duty, but he knew it was also a privilege and a blessing. Hope is just as necessary today as it was for Peter's congregation. Peter believed that focusing on and looking forward to the fulfillment of God's promises was important in preparing his people for suffering.

In order to help his people develop true hope, Peter had his people recall the *already*—they were God's children and heirs with an inheritance. This change would motivate them to focus on the sure and certain *not yet* in their time of hardship and trouble (verses 3-5). Remember that the term *not yet* refers to that which has been promised and secured by Christ but awaits its final fulfillment. Proper living in the *already* requires a proper focus on the *not yet*. Part of the *not yet* is the coming glories of the believer's salvation and inheritance to be revealed at Christ's return (verses 3-9).

Christ will bring the blessings and riches of total sanctification (glorification) and the inexpressible privilege and wonder of seeing God. *Not yet* living is living in the present with an eternal perspective. The believer focuses on Heaven and the glory to be revealed because he has a piece of the Triune God, due to his relationship with Christ by the Holy Spirit. The believer has begun resurrection life at salvation, and he lives with and in the hope of full glory. True hope is necessary for living with an eternal perspective, pleasing the Triune God, imitating Christ, and experiencing the joy of living as a child of the King.[9]

In these verses (3-5), Peter, in a true hope-engendering way, reminded his people that the Triune God was the *Bequeather*, who had heirs—individually and corporately—and a guaranteed inheritance—Heaven—which would never perish, spoil, or fade. Since the *Bequeather* does not change, God and His promises can be trusted. The inheritance and the Triune's God's heirs will not be lost. The Triune God guaranteed the source of true hope—Himself—by highlighting what He had done, was doing, and will do.

Peter outlined the Triune God's activity who, among other things, had called the people—His heirs—into a living hope through the resurrection of Christ. That living hope consisted of their inheritance—Heaven—which they had *now/already* but

---

9   This is part of Paul's emphasis in Philippians 4:13: *I can do all things through Christ that strengthens me*. Paul's "already living" included "doing all things." By "doing all things" he meant living in poverty or riches and doing so by honoring God (4:10-12). "Doing all things" is using whatever circumstance a believer finds himself in to grow into Christlikeness. He does that by applying biblical truth as a means of imitating Christ.

not fully. If the inheritance was being kept and preserved, so, too, were the heirs! The inheritance is being kept, maintained, and guarded in Heaven, awaiting the arrival of believers (Hebrews 6:19-20). The hope is a living hope based on the reality of the living God—His presence, power, promises, plan, purposes, and provisions for His people. The Triune God is the author of a perfect and true faith and hope which is radically different from the dead, counterfeit hope associated with the worship and allegiance to false, dead gods.

In verses 6-9, Peter encouraged the congregation to rejoice amidst hard times (God's providence) because God had a purpose for their faith: the fullness of their salvation. Again, Peter pictured the *already*—salvation and heirs and an inheritance—which was theirs and would pay dividends as they experienced more and more the fullness of their salvation amid hard times. The *not yet* would come—but not yet!

Peter called the people to act based on true hope by thinking and conducting themselves with an *already* but *not yet* mindset. As believers they had proper knowledge: the truth of the gospel in Christ by the Holy Spirit as well as the truth about themselves as saved sinners and the God who saved them. They had the proper position; they were saints, which means *called out ones* (Romans 1:7; 1 Corinthians 1:2). They had the proper provisions: a new heart, union with Christ—they were in Christ; and they were indwelt by the Holy Spirit (John 3:3-8; 2 Corinthians 5:17;

Ephesians 1:4; Romans 8:9-11). On earth, they were living in the *already* awaiting the *not yet*. They were not home in Heaven with God, but they were told to anticipate it as a means of living in the *now/already*; in that sense, they were living in the *not yet*. Peter juxtaposed the two as a means of giving true hope. Thus, Peter encouraged his people to set their hope not on what is seen by physical eyes but on what is seen by spiritual eyes (2 Corinthians 5:7; Paul refers to this as saving faith). Peter defined their hope and taught them how to apply it. He had experiences in both—initially as a loser, but later as a victor (Mark 14:66-72; John 21:15-19). Peter had tasted the Triune God's covenantal faithfulness. He enjoyed it and he wanted his people to enjoy the same pleasure and victory (Psalm 34:8).

Peter concluded his introduction (verses 1-2, 3-12) with a graphic call to action based on the truth taught in those opening verses. His people were amidst trouble that would intensify. In verse 13, Peter, loud and clear, gave the call for them to set their hope entirely on God and His grace. Peter was concerned that the people had or would set their hope on something else. He knew that man was created a hope-based being. He had personal experience with the importance of true hope and endurance based on that hope (Matthew 26:35; Mark 14:31; Luke 22:31-34).

Peter taught believers of all ages that hope is relational, and as such, it is a gift (there is hope)! As such, viewing God, self, and God's providence from a perspective of true hope is a choice—it is a matter of the will based on proper knowledge. Again, as a reminder, God doesn't give His people commands that they are unable to keep. If hope is commanded, hope must be attainable and of utmost importance to God and His people. Further, if the Triune God has commanded hope and unbelievers don't have it, then God must have provided it for His people. If He provides it, then true hope is a reality to be grasped and enjoyed.

Application

1. What hope does Peter give in 1 Peter 1:13, and what is its significance?

2. What can we learn about true hope?

3. What were the circumstances surrounding Peter's command?

4. What personal experience did he have with hope and how did he do?

5. Regarding true hope, how must your thinking and wanting change?

CHAPTER 6

The Triune God's Provision of True Hope

THE TRIUNE GOD IS THE *source* of all hope (Romans 15:4, 13).[10] Moreover, Jesus in the believer is the hope of glory and the Holy Spirit pours the Triune God's love and hope into the heart of believers (Colossians 1:27; Romans 5:5). These simple statements are profound. They express Intratrinitarian activity. True hope has no other source. The Triune God defines hope, places Himself at the center of true hope, and is the Giver of all good gifts, including hope. The Triune God is the Source of all hope because, (don't miss this point) He is the God of all hope. Not only is God the author and Perfector of our faith (Hebrews 12:1-3), He is the Fountainhead and Author of all hope. Not only is God love and the Source and Originator of all love, He is the Fountainhead of all hope (1 John 4:7-8), which He gives in abundance through the Spirit. Again, faith,

---

10   Romans 15:4, 13: *"Whatever was written before was written for our instruction that by endurance and the encouragement that the Scriptures give us, we may have hope." "Now may the God of all hope fill you with every sort of joy and peace in believing, so that you may have an abundance of hope by the power of the Holy Spirit."*

hope, and love are evidence of the Triune God at work in the believer. If love and faith are gifts from God, so, too, is hope.

Look again at how the Triune God provided hope. He saved a believer when he was an unbeliever and an enemy by placing him in Christ, *and* our God made the Son to be the hope of all believers. The term "in Christ" is a unique and especially Pauline term that indicates the believer is supernaturally and miraculously in proper relationship to Christ. As a result, the believer has access to everything Christ has because he is united to Him (Romans 5:2; Ephesians 2:18; 3:12; Hebrews 10:19-22). The Triune God has established a personal, one-on-one relationship with the Christian so that Christ becomes the believer's hope (Colossians 1:27; 1 Timothy 1:1; Hebrews 12:1-3; 6:18-20).

The believer has true hope because he has a sure foundation for that hope—Jesus Christ, the resurrected, ascended, and interceding Savior (Romans 8:9-11, 34; Hebrews 7:25; 9:24). Christ has demonstrated and affirmed that the Triune God is the trustworthy and the ultimate Promise-keeper. Not only that, the believer is indwelt with the Holy Spirit Who gives him a new orientation, capacity, inclination, and disposition to put off false hope and put on biblical hope (Ephesians 2:1-3, 4, 5-10). True hope doesn't disappoint (Romans 5:5).

True hope comes without disappointment and comes mainly from the blessing that nobody wants—trouble. Trouble, per se, is not a blessing. It is part of the curse. Rather, it is the context for the person to express the significance of his relationship with the Triune God. The person's response is based on his identity in Christ and the significance it plays in the believer's life. The word translated "affliction" is *thlipsis,* which means trouble of any and every kind. The culture refers to God's providence as "stress" or "pressure." The picture this creates is a person being squeezed from the outside. The Bible paints a different picture. Every person is a player in a moral drama in his own heart, played out in daily life. God in His providence places people in various situations. These situations, however, don't cause the person's response. They are the milieu for the person to live out his faith, hope, and love based on his relationship with the Triune God.

The hope that doesn't disappoint is vitally connected with one's relationship in Christ and its importance to the person. Only the believer will use trouble to develop Christlikeness. His response confirms God's purpose to sanctify His people and is proof of the believer's new condition, standing, and position in Christ. Hope is produced and acknowledged because of the knowledge that one has been radically transformed by grace. The believer observes evidence of that transformation in his life as well as in the lives of other believers. This evidence and its fruit confirm and affirm the Triune God's hope-producing activity in the believer. Hope looks away from self to the God of grace and His greatness.

The believer is truly a new creature in Christ in the new creation (2 Corinthians 5:17).[11] Therefore, there is hope in God and His Word for any and all problems. True hope focuses on the believer honoring God and not necessarily getting what he wants. The believer is looking for God's solution to trouble. To reiterate, true hope is necessary for living with a proper Godly perspective of and in the *already/now*. But true hope doesn't come to the believer apart from Scripture and the Holy Spirit. True hope is never zapped in magically or somehow mystically acquired. You and I can expect (true hope!) that the Holy Spirit will work as He promised—in us and with us through the Word but never for us, against us, or apart from the Word.

Please catch the greatness of our God. The Triune God defines hope, places Himself at the center of that hope, establishes the Son as the foundation for true hope, and gives hope abundantly through the Spirit and His Word. God is the Source of all hope because (don't miss this point) He is the God of all hope.

The Triune God has made the Son to be the hope of all believers, and He made unbelievers into believers (we call this salvation which occurred at the time of regeneration: John 3:3-8) by placing them in Christ. Being in Christ means

---

11   2 Corinthians 5:17: *Accordingly, if anyone is in Christ, he is a new creation; the old has passed away; see, new things have come into being.*

that one is in a relationship with Him and is indwelt by the Holy Spirit, the Spirit of truth (John 14:17; 15:26; 16:13; Romans 8:11). The believer has access to everything Christ has because he is united with Him (Romans 5:1-2; Ephesians 2:18; 3:12). When these supernatural, Intratrinitarian-originated and sustained activities occur in the heart of the now-believer, Christ becomes the believer's hope (Romans 5:5; 8:24-26; 15:4, 13; Colossians 1:27). The believer has true hope, which is the blessed assurance that God is the Promise-maker and Promise-keeper. This is a non-negotiable fact and reality. The believer ignores this fact at his own peril and misery. The believer has the sure foundation for hope—the Triune God, as evidenced by Christ's mediatorial work and the Holy Spirit's application of His work. As a result, the believer develops more and more Christlikeness, which includes dying to self by living to and for God.

Just as Jesus Christ is the Way, the Truth and the Life (John 14:6), so, too, true hope is the Person—Jesus Christ. The person and work of Jesus Christ is the only basis for God's kind of hope. The indwelling Holy Spirit brings to light these truths so that the believer is never without true hope (Romans 8:23-27).

True hope is manifested in any number of ways. It is the companion of saving faith. As a result, pleasing God in thoughts, desires, and actions becomes one of the believer's mottoes for this earthly life—the *already* and the *now*. Life is thus simplified, and choices clarified. One can always try to please God, no matter His providence.

Application

1. Hope is knowledge-dependent, relational, a gift, a necessity, and a choice. Do you agree or disagree and why?
2. Hope is commanded. How is that possible?
3. Who or what is the Fountainhead of all hope? What significance should and does that have for you and why?

CHAPTER 7

Saving Faith and True Hope: Twin Pillars Of and For Godly Living

AN IMPORTANT COROLLARY POINT FOR understanding true hope is a proper understanding of the relationship between saving faith and true hope. Often both occur together in the Bible (Romans 5:1-5; Galatians 5:5-6; 1 Thessalonians 1:3; 5:8). There is no hope without saving faith in Christ Jesus, since saving faith and true hope are rooted in Him. Saving faith would be empty and futile without true hope and true hope would have no foundation without saving faith. You can't separate the two because both have their foundation in the Triune God—His promises and power. Both have the same object and the same content but approach the Triune God and the Christian life from a different perspective.

Saving faith and true hope have the same focus: God's trustworthiness as the Promise-Maker and Promise-Keeper. Saving faith is based on the certainty of the fulfillment of what God has promised. True hope is the sure anticipation and the certain expectation of that fulfillment. Hope enables the believer to look forward to the certain fulfillment of what God has faithfully promised. Saving faith gives rise to the certainty that true hope's expectation has been, is being, and will be fulfilled.

The writer of Hebrews brings faith and hope together: *Now faith is a solidly grounded certainty about what we hope for, a conviction about the reality of things we don't see* (11:1). Said another way, saving faith is a solidly grounded certainty about what we hope for and expect to be fulfilled, and that hope's expectation will be fulfilled. True hope, like faith, is the conviction—a strong, justified, true belief—about the reality that things not seen, but proclaimed in the Bible, will be fulfilled. Both faith and hope involve knowledge and have a cognitive element to them.

Saving faith has true hope as a major constituent. The two are built on and fortify each other. You can't have one without the other. Each gives a perspective. Saving faith looks at the unseen (future, end results, and that which is unknown to man but not to God) with God's "eyes" or from God's perspective as given in His word. True hope focuses on saving faith's object. It focuses on what the believer does not have *now* but on the believer's final product which is being worked on *now*. It enables the believer to believe, expect, and trust God and what He has promised *now*. True hope has an eternal perspective so that the *now* is seen through the perspective of the *not yet*. Both saving faith and true hope relate back to God and are grounded in His covenantal faithfulness and the content of God's promises.

If you have been tracking with me, you should agree that it is proper to talk about a person possessing true or false hope rather than having hope or no hope. If one has true hope, he will never be hopeless. The reason rests in Christ. True hope is Jesus Christ as revealed by the Spirit (Romans 5:5; 8:9-11; Colossians 1:27; 1 Timothy 1:1; Hebrews 12:1-3). In the context of Paul's letter to the Colossians, he wrote in 1:27: *those to whom, God wished to make known what are the riches of the glory of this secret among the Gentiles which is Christ in you, the hope of glory . . .*

What does it mean: *Christ in you the hope of glory*? In the context of Paul's letter to the Colossians, he was refuting false teaching, especially that of pagan philosophies concerning Jesus. In verse 27 of chapter 1, Paul writes that the Triune God wished to make known (publicly declare) the mystery of the riches of His glory among the Gentiles, which had been hidden in ages past. This mystery was Christ, the Savior of both Gentile and Jew (Ephesians 2:11-15; 3:3-6, 7-13). Now, God revealed in Christ's first coming that He had fulfilled His promise first made to Adam and Eve in Genesis 3:15 and subsequently given to Abraham and repeated through the centuries (Genesis 12:3-7). Christ is the hope of glory because the Triune God brings sinners from every tribe, tongue, people, and nation under His one roof—His family and kingdom. It is in this sense that the gospel is universal—the two (Jew and Gentile) became one (Ephesians 2:11-15). This is a source of great hope and trust for believers of all ages. The hope is both for salvation and life after salvation. Please don't miss the last point. Being and living as one saved is a package deal!

Paul also wrote that Jesus Christ, our hope of glory, is "in" or "among you." Paul points to the presence of Christ. Jesus is present with His people (Matthew 1:23: Immanuel: *God with us*; Luke 17:21). Christ is present with His people and Church via the Holy Spirit (Ephesians 1:14-19; 3:14-19). Therefore, hope is based on the victorious, ever-present God. Believers are victors because Christ is the ultimate Victor and they are in Him. He came, completed the appointed work of the Triune God, returned to His rightful place of preeminence, and promised to return.[12] He came, saw, and conquered—even though His own considered Him a loser! Therefore, believers are guaranteed victory so that hope is a certainty. The believer's hope is based on the facts: Christ came, conquered, rose, ascended into Heaven as the winner and the true Victor and He will return (Romans 8:35-37).

---

12   Victory is defined as overcoming. The once-for-all victory for every believer came when Jesus lived perfectly and died perfectly on the cross as the Perfect Sacrifice. The debt had been paid in full and all hostility between God and man was removed. There was no condemnation for the believer. Therefore, daily victory for the Christian is a reality. Victory is becoming more like Christ daily in thoughts, desires, and actions. The believer is victorious when he is controlled by biblical principles rather than the agony of the problem and his wants. Said another way, victory is using what a person doesn't like as an instrument for growth into Christlikeness. Victory is pleasing God even when it seems and feels impossible and one rather than seek relief.

Before Christ left, He sent the Holy Spirit to dwell in believers individually and corporately (John 14:25-26; 15:26-27; 16:13). Christ is with believers in the Person of the Holy Spirit (1 Corinthians 3:16-17; 6:15-20; 2 Corinthians 6:14-16). Believers are and can be victorious because Christ was and is victorious. The Father's acceptance of Jesus' mediatorial work and proof of Jesus' victory is His resurrection and the indwelling of the Holy Spirit (Romans 4:25).

The Pauline passages discussed in this section refer to the wisdom and glory of God in Christ by the Holy Spirit for His people. Consider these hope-engendering truths. Loving and saving unlovely people who were His enemies is nothing short of glorious and mind-boggling (Romans 5:6-10)! That is part of the *already*. Yet there is more to come: there is the glory to be revealed when Jesus returns—part of the *not yet*. It is an understatement to say that when Jesus returns it will be something to behold (Revelation 1:7-8; also see 1 Thessalonians 2:19; 4:16-17).

True hope is founded in and on a Person, and every believer has this hope because he has Christ, or more accurately, Christ has him. Every believer has true hope as a gift from the Triune God: in Him and through Him, now and for eternity. Since Jesus is eternal and unchangeable, so, too, is the believer's hope. This hope is not a *hope so* or *maybe*. It is the real thing—solid and true. As a result, the believer's hope is not dependent on circumstances and what others do or don't do. That fact alone is liberating because a Christian is not tied to circumstances or other people. Rather, he and his hope are grounded in the very Person and work of the Triune God. The believer's hope is in the God of the circumstances and what He is doing in them. As he focuses on the Triune God and His purposes, the believer develops increasing Christlikeness, one of the reasons God saved us (Romans 8:28-29; Ephesians 1:4).

In Christ, believers recognize evidence of the *already* and *not yet*. *Already* and *now* He is with believers and His Church in the Person of the Holy Spirit (1 Corinthians 3:16; 6:19-20; 2 Corinthians 6:16). Believers are victorious because Christ was and is victorious. By and through the Holy Spirit, the Immanuel (God with us) principle is a reality. Future and final victory will be signaled by Christ's second coming. The expectation, conviction, and certainty of a realized, final, future victory are the road to present-day victory.

Looking ahead to future victory in the midst of perilous times motivated John (1 John 3:1-3) and Paul to live and minister, for God's glory and the good of the people (Colossians 1:28-29). Difficult times were and are part of the *now*—living in a fallen world (John 15:18-21; 2 Corinthians 4:8-10; 6:4-10; 11:23-29). What was true of Paul's motivation should be true for every believer through the ages, including you and me.

Similarly, as previously discussed (Chapter 5), Peter thought true hope was so important that he commands the soon to-be-suffering saints to set their hope fully on the glory that is to be revealed when Jesus returns (1 Peter 1:13). Peter knew that true hope rests on God's presence, power, and promises. These promises, like God Himself, are unchangeable and forever (1 Peter 1:3-5). God and His promises are a firm rock on which to stand. Hope provides endurance and without it, people are hopeless. Hopeless people are those who lack or fail to grasp true hope; their hope is no hope at all. They grow weary and don't finish the race—they do not endure and will never gain the crown of life (1 Thessalonians 1:3; 2 Timothy 4:7-8; Hebrews 12:1-3).

As previously mentioned, Peter thought this forward look so important that he commanded the soon-to-be-suffering saints to set their hopes fully on the glory that is to be revealed when Jesus returns (1 Peter 1:13). Peter knew that true hope rested on God and His promises. These promises, like God Himself, are unchangeable and forever, a firm rock on which to stand. Hope provides endurance and without it, people are hopeless. Hopeless people are those who lack true hope, grow weary, and don't finish the race (1 Thessalonians 1:3; Hebrews 12:1-3).

In summary, we have learned that fallen man has hopes and expectations that focus on what he thinks will make him happy. The Bible teaches that every person is tied or linked representatively to Adam. Therefore, what Adam did in the Garden, God considered every person born by ordinary generation (Jesus Christ was born of a virgin) to have done. So, when Adam placed his concerns before and above pleasing God (Genesis 3:1-6), this led to each of his descendants doing the same. All people are, at heart, self-pleasers with false hopes and expectations. As stated earlier, only God's salvation can bring about a change in man's orientation, hope, and focus.

Application

1. Based on Hebrews 11:1-6 what is the connection between saving faith and true hope?
2. What is the *already* of saving faith and true hope? See Colossians 1:27.
3. What is the *not yet*?
4. What are some of the promises of God that are foundational for saving faith and true hope?
5. What is your relation to those promises and how do you rely on them?

CHAPTER 8

A Comparison of True and False Hope: Similarities and Differences Between True Hope and Saving Faith

THE BIBLE TEACHES THAT THE culture and the world (defined as the people and the system that are pro-self, anti-God, and have suppressed and attempted to replace His truth with their own foolishness) hope one way, while believers hope another way. In the opening paragraphs of the book, I established the biblical principle of discernment as the means by which one would compare true and false hope. We have noted that the Bible sets forth the doctrine of two ways: saved and unsaved, lost and found, light and darkness, and clean and unclean. As an application of this teaching, Paul sets out true hope and false hope in the context of grief and despair and describes the difference in 1 Thessalonians 4:13 (*Brothers, we don't want you to be ignorant brothers about those who sleep, or to grieve like the rest men who have no hope*).

Paul describes the difference in order to minister to the congregation in Thessalonica. They misunderstood Christ's first coming, His going, and His return. Their loved ones were dying and had died and there was no Christ. Paul, using the context of concern for those who have died before Jesus' return, encouraged and exhorted the congregation to grieve God's way! Godly grieving is based in part on true hope.

Paul cites God's promise in verse fourteen as the object of their faith and hope: *We believe that Jesus died and rose again, and so we believe that God will bring with Jesus those who have asleep in him.* The object of their faith and hope should be the resurrected Lord, which is a non-negotiable truth and an essential element of God's guarantee that He will take care of those who die before Jesus returns.

Paul teaches his people then and now that grief without hope is despair. Grief without hope is jettisoning the object of saving and true hope—Jesus Christ, the hope of glory. If there is no Christ, there is no resurrected Christ and there is no foundation for the gospel and saving faith and true hope (1 Corinthians 15:19). Everyone is doomed to misery in this life, but eternal misery is true hopelessness! Paul presented the facts and the congregation had to answer a simple yet profound question: did they believe and accept these facts as true?

Grief is an unavoidable part of living in a fallen world; despair is not. Moreover, grieving (please note the difference between the noun and the verb) is a necessary part of living in a fallen world, but again, despairing is not. Grief comes as a result of pain and misery, which entered the world as a result of God's judgment for the initial sin of Adam (Genesis 3:15-17; Romans 5:12-14; 2 Corinthians 4:16-18). It is the by-product of God's judgment and curse. Grieving is a response to the misery and its results. It is always right to acknowledge the source of grief in order to grieve God's way. Despair is the result of false hope and is based on ignorance and, perhaps, arrogance. However, the hope of the believer is in Christ and His promises. True hope enables the believer to view the circumstances through biblical truth and not doubt God during hard times.

According to 1 Thessalonians 4:13, despair is based on ignorance of God's truth. Hopeless people despair because their hope has failed them. The congregation misunderstood God's truth. The people lived as if Christ had failed (see Luke 24:13-35). He had not returned, and people were dead. Despair was associated with ignorance and misunderstanding. In contrast, because the hope of the believer is in Christ and His promises, the Christian grieves properly. His hope is an anchor that keeps him from drifting into despair (Hebrews 6:18-20).[13]

The fallen man has hopes and expectations that focus on what he thinks will make him happy. Why is that? Basically,

---

13   Hebrews 6:18-20: *The result was that by two unchangeable things, in which it is impossible for God to lie, we who have fled for protection might have strong encouragement to lay hold of the hope set before us. We have this hope as a safe and secure anchor for the soul; it is one that enters into the place on the inner side of the curtain where Jesus has entered as a Forerunner on our behalf by becoming an eternal High Priest after the order of Melchizedek.*

that is what Adam did! The Bible teaches that every person is "tied" representatively to Adam. Therefore, what Adam did in the Garden, God considered that we did. When Adam placed himself and his concerns before pleasing God (Genesis 3:1-6), every descendant did also. Thus, and I repeat, every person is, at heart, a self-pleaser. Only a radical inner man, heart transformation can bring about a changed motivation, orientation, and focus. This radical change is called regeneration, which leads to salvation. Prior to that time, taking care of oneself was preeminent in a person's thinking. Knowing this fact will help us as we contrast true and false hope.

I return to our two definitions of true and false hope. False hope is defined as *a personal attitude of expectation of possible fulfillment for the right now that is an uncertain hope-so.* Remember, biblical hope is defined as *the personal attitude of a confident, sure expectation, and anticipation of something good.* It is based on knowing that God makes promises, that He keeps those promises, and that the believer is a recipient of those promises—both now and eternally. The operative words in each definition include attitude or thinking, expectation and anticipation, and focus or object.

In studying hope in this manner, it is informative to quickly review the biblical view of saving faith. Both faith and hope have three aspects: knowledge or cognition, desire, and action. We must remember that everyone was created a faith-based and hope-based being. As such, man has faith but not salvation.

Non-saving faith is *belief in man's ability to take care of himself now by his own resources and reasoning, with or without a view toward his final destiny*. It looks to self, for self, and by self, even if the object of faith is another person. On the other hand, saving faith looks away from self and to God. Faith, saving and non-saving is composed of at least three elements. These include cognition (*notitia*), conviction (*assensus*), and commitment (*fiducia*), which results in another "C" word: confidence. These elements emphasize that faith involves the whole man—both the inner man and outer man. Saving faith involves knowledge (cognition) of a person, Jesus Christ, and not merely knowing facts about Him. That knowledge includes Who He was and what He did while on the earth as the Godman. It also involves knowledge of self: origin, identity, purpose, and destiny.

Saving faith also involves that aspect of the inner man called the affections or desires. I equate the two, although others speak of affections as involving emotions while others refer to affections as a function of the will. Man must be convicted of his sin (sin and man's separation from God is the bad news of man's condition), of his sinfulness, and of the saving grace of God through His Son (the gospel message is God's good news) by the Holy Spirit. Saving faith also involves the will. There must be a commitment to turning from self, sin, and Satan to

God, which results in willful and purposeful acts to confirm the commitment. Consider this example: a person knows the chair and believes the chair can hold him up. But unless he sits in the chair (an act of the will based on the conviction that what is said about the chair is true), he doesn't truly believe in the chair's ability.

Hope follows the same pattern: thoughts, desires, and actions (or commitment). Both true hope and false hope involve attitudes, beliefs, and thoughts. Like faith, hope is grounded in certain facts that result in thoughts, beliefs, attitudes, and perspectives. Don't miss the point that there is a cognitive aspect of hope. Hope is based on knowledge followed by the conviction that his hope is solid. The person holds on to that hope—he is committed to it. He pursues its fulfillment.

False hope is based on knowledge unaided by and ungrounded in biblical truth. It is based on human wisdom and a perspective of life that relies on a feeling orientation (what feels right or doesn't feel right) and/or experience. A person with false hope has convinced himself that his hope is satisfactory and that he is doing the best he can by some standard other than God's. True hope is based on biblical truth implemented God's way (Romans 5:1-5; James 1:2-4; 1 Peter 1:6-8).

True hope is based on what a person knows and not on what he feels nor his circumstances and experiences. The person with false hope thinks and declares, "I have to have what I think and know will make me happy." Happiness is a feeling usually based on a desire for a better life, "ease and relief," and better feelings usually unrelated to the God of circumstances. In contradistinction, the person with true hope thinks and says, "Pleasing God is my aim and ambition in life because I have a relationship with the risen Lord by the Holy Spirit who dwells in me and the Church. I will think differently about myself and others in this situation." Moreover, he counsels himself with the truth that "Pleasing God is my source of joy, satisfaction, and contentment because God created and re-created me for this" (John 4:31-34; 2 Corinthians 5:9-15; Psalm 73:23-26).

Jesus Christ epitomized this approach to life and believers are to imitate him. In 2 Corinthians 5:14-15, Paul wrote that the love of Christ motivates and compels him to please God rather than self.[14] This motivation is the exact opposite of that which drives someone who has false hope. That person often expects and even demands that God should treat him better than He did Christ!

Also, there is a willful aspect of hope. Both true hope and false hope involve a willful and purposeful choice. People are choosers. Because people are commanded to hope, hope involves a choice, a duty, and a privilege (1 Peter 1:13). Where and how a person sets his hope can be taught, learned, and

---

14   2 Corinthians 5:9, 14-15: *So then whether at home or away from home, we make it our ambition to please Him. The love of Christ is our motivation since we judge as follows: One died for all; therefore all have died. He died for all so that those who live might live no longer for themselves, but rather for the One Who died and rose for them.*

practiced. An example of this is given in 1 Corinthians 15. Paul was teaching the reality and importance of the bodily resurrection of Christ and of the believers. In verses 19-20, Paul taught a remarkable truth that turned the culture's perspective upside down and forced the Christian to reconsider his idea of hope.[15] Paul writes that those who set their hope in and on Christ for this life only (the right *now*) are to be pitied above all others, and he gives two reasons: the present life is vanity and there is an eternal destiny (the *not yet*). They have no vision of the *not yet*. The right *now* is temporary, but there is an eternal joy for those saved that begins *now* for the believer (the *already*).

The joy of salvation begins now and continues into eternity. Life is simplified when there is an eternal perspective. There is direction, confidence, and joy because no matter God's control and His providence, pleasing God is a reality and a source of joy and peace. Jesus demonstrated this truth throughout His ministry as He moved to the cross (Hebrews 12:1-3).

The *not yet* is the permanent and incorruptible life as a resurrected son (glorification) just as Jesus has life as the Resurrected Son (Romans 6:9-10).[16] The believer has a piece of

---

15   1 Corinthians 15:19-20: *If we have hope in Christ only for this life, then we are to be pitied above all persons. But the fact is that Christ has been raised from the dead, the First Fruits of those who are sleeping.*

16   Romans 6:9-10: *Knowing that since Christ has been raised from the dead He won't ever die again; death no longer holds lordship over Him. The death that He died, He died to sin once, forever, but the life that he lives, He lives for God.*

the *not yet* while on earth because he is saved. As I have written, but it is worth repeating, resurrection life begins at salvation and union with Christ (John 17:3). John and Paul commented on these truths. They lived as resurrected people because they had an eternal perspective (Colossians 3:1-3; 1 John 3:1-3).

Expectation and Anticipation: Key Ingredients

Faith and hope also have an expectation and anticipation as key ingredients. True hope means that the person is convinced—he knows—that God is trustworthy and that He is faithful to His covenant promises: He makes and keeps His promises which are *yes* in Christ by the Holy Spirit: 2 Corinthians 1:20-22). Because God can be counted on to keep His promises, true hope is a firmly grounded certainty. Believers are to be growing as trusting saints because God is trustworthy.

The Christian should expect for and anticipate God to keep His promises. Redemptive history gives evidence of His covenantal faithfulness. In the believer's earthly life, true hope enables him to view his growth into Christlikeness as a preview and foretaste of eternal life. True hope always looks toward the final victory in Christ and Heaven, but in such a way that the believer is of earthly good. True hope brings Heaven to the believer and helps him eagerly anticipate the glory of the Triune God in Christ. Consider this example. Going to Grandmother's house is usually an exciting time. Anticipation and eager expectation abounds. Activity in the house prior to leaving is accelerated. The family is abuzz before and in the car. The anticipation increases as the family nears their destination. This simple example sheds light on the believer in the *already* or the *now*. Living this life with both an eye on and foot in Heaven should motivate the believer to live as a child of the King.

True hope's expectation is holiness rather than happiness, which is the goal of false hope. God's holiness means He is set apart from all His creatures. Holiness for the believer means he is set apart from himself and given to God. That includes being set apart from the world defined as a world opposed to God either overtly or covertly. God desires and commands His children to be holy and blameless as His Son is (Ephesians 1:4; 1 Peter 1:16; Matthew 5:48).[17] God has done marvelous and supernatural things in order to guarantee that this holiness occurs, thereby giving true hope:

1. He gave His Son, Who lived a perfect life and died a perfect death, to be the crucified Savior.

2. Jesus did not stay in the ground. Not only is He the crucified Savior, He is the Resurrected, exalted Savior at the place of preeminence in Heaven.

---

17   Ephesians 1:4: *Even as He chose us in Him before the foundation of the world to be holy and blameless before Him . . .* ; 1 Peter 1:16: *I say this because it is written: you must be holy because I am holy.* Matthew 5:48: *So then, you must be perfect as your heavenly Father is perfect.*

3. He placed each saved person in Christ by the Holy Spirit at regeneration.

4. He sent the Holy Spirit to dwell in the hearts of every child of God as down payment for the believer's eternal dwelling with Him (Romans 5:5; 2 Corinthians 1:20-22; Ephesians 1:13-14).

5. He preserved His Word—the Bible—for His people.

6. He perseveres His people via His covenantal faithfulness. The promise that runs throughout the Old Testament is true throughout the ages: *I am your God and you are my people* (Exodus 6:7; 19:5-6; Leviticus 26:12; 1 Peter 2:4-10).

7. He has promised to never leave or forsake His people and He has kept His Word (Deuteronomy 31:6, 8; Joshua 1:9).

In contrast, false hope has no firm foundation. It is only for the *now*—this present life. It rests on the expectation of happiness defined according to the logic of a world system opposed to God and views happenings as something owed to him as a vehicle for his happiness defined by and as good feelings and ease. However, in this life and in this world, *your way* and what the world would call happiness is never guaranteed. False hope, then, is only a *hope-so* characterized as *wishful thinking, maybe, perhaps, not sure*, and *no guarantee*. False hope may or may not be realized, and if it is, it isn't long lasting. It is "here today and gone tomorrow."

The expectation of true hope has both a vertical (looking to God) and horizontal (man to man) dimension. Vertically, the Christian with true hope looks to God as the trustworthy Promise-Maker and Promise-Keeper and trusts Him. Trust is demonstrated in the believer's life in a myriad of ways. He remembers specific truths about God and himself that motivate him to endure God's way. I discuss these in greater detail in the last chapters. False hope has no proper vertical dimension; its goal is getting what a person believes will make him feel better and happy.

True hope's horizontal dimension means that all of God's people will look upon themselves and others differently. Since people and things and what they give or don't give are never a Christian's source or basis for hope, the believer will not covet and use people, or God, for his purposes. Rather, the Christian will consider others more important than himself and will put another's interest above his own (Philippians 2:3-4).[18] In this way, true hope is contagious so that others are carried along looking toward the God of hope.

Faith and Hope Have an Object and Focus

Also, like faith, hope has an object and focus. False hope focuses on the present, the personal, the visible, the external,

---

18   Philippians 2:3-4: *Do nothing out of selfishness or vanity, but rather in humility consider others better than yourselves. Each of you should not only look out for his own interests but also the interests of others.*

the created and the temporal (what I have termed right *now* living). Each of these words conjures pictures of life that is dependent on one's own understanding of what is important and valuable (Matthew 6:19-24; 1 Corinthians 15:19-20). In this sense, the person who is a sensual being is informed by what is happening around him. However, he is using a faulty interpretative grid.

An unbeliever's (and a believer who is functioning as an unbeliever) interpretative grid is feelings, reason divorced from biblical truth, his own experience, circumstances, and/ or practical, common sense. In this sense (no pun intended!), man a sensual being and is informed by what is happening around him, but he is using a faulty interpretative grid. His senses are intact, but his interpretative grid is false. Therefore, his conclusions are not God-honoring. In fact, he competes with God. He lives in God's world as a rebel.

Too often, the believer can function from the same mindset and in the same manner. For instance, this person may be criticized properly or improperly. True hope pushes the believer to evaluate what is said in light of growth in Christ. He will keep himself open to change. He will discard what is flawed biblically.

The unbeliever has no other option but to rebel, sometimes not-so-subtly and at other times in less obvious ways. His understanding is darkened and dead to the things of God but alive to self. His desires are self-oriented, and his focus is right *now*—on the here and *now* for self. He interprets what he sees, tastes, touches, and hears based on the interpretative grid of right *now* for self. *Me* is center stage. This is sinful *sensual-sensory* living! The person has divorced himself from God's truth; he attempted to exchange it with his own system of reasoning (Romans 1:18-23). This exchange is the initial step of idolatry—the creature arrogantly and ignorantly attempts to substitute himself for the Creator. He attempts to push God off the throne. The focus of sinful, sensual living is on the personal, which is highlighted by an attitude of: "What is in it for me—right *now*?" Or "What makes me happy, right *now*." False hope focuses on and expects a quick fix to problems, which is only superficial, temporary, or is no solution at all.

In contrast, true hope focuses on Christ Who is the believer's hope of glory (Colossians 1:27). True hope does not ignore the *now* but views it from a different perspective. True hope enables the believer to use his senses in a God-pleasing manner. He has a sensual experience and interprets the *now* through the *already* (what he is in Christ) and *not yet* (what is in store eternally). By design and necessity, true hope looks beyond self—the personal, the present circumstances, and the right *now*—to the God of circumstances and His provisions and solution. True hope focuses on a Person and it is not self—it is the Triune God as Creator, Controller, Sustainer, and Owner of His world and the creatures in it. God's promises are true, yes and amen, in Christ by the Holy Spirit because Jesus Christ and the Holy Spirit are true to themselves and to the Triune God (2 Corinthians 1:20-22; 5:5; Ephesians 1:14). That is hope-engendering.

True hope is *suprasensual,* meaning that the believer understands and views life through the eyes of biblical truth and saving faith, which is anchored in God, His promises, and His faithfulness. Saving faith and true hope are the interpretative grid by which the believer evaluates "life"— God's providential control. Only the believer has a change in his interpretative grid which occurred supernaturally at regeneration. The believer's interpretative grid is no longer founded on what he takes in via the senses, unaided by biblical truths. He views "life"—God's providence and the meaning of life—through the lens of biblical truth and God's presence, promises, power, purpose, plan, program, and provisions. In this way, true hope rests on the Triune God and His promises. His promises are true because He is true.

When a person looks at his circumstances and happenings and evaluates them via the biblical grid of experience, feelings, and unaided human reasoning, he draws conclusions about God, himself, and his situation. This is what characterizes sinful, sensual living. Since he is not moored to and by biblical truth, he will not discover and develop true hope. He can expect misery in this life and the next. Some people think they can "read God" from circumstances. When they do, they are depending on their own understanding rather than the Word of God. Human reasoning and feelings are no match for God's wisdom (1 Corinthians 1:18-31). Rather, God is the God of circumstances and that makes all the difference.

Consider David's response to Goliath in 1 Samuel 17. It was no tall order (no pun intended!) for him to view Goliath through God's perspective rather than his own. Because he practiced suprasensual living, he accomplished God's purpose when King Saul and the entire army of Israel had failed. David knew that it was God's world and that He had promised to be with His people. David had a sensual experience. He saw the enemy and what was at stake. He took in information but evaluated it suprasensually—through the eyes or grid of God's truth via saving faith and true hope. He knew facts about himself and the enemy. He concluded that the battle was God's and that he was Yahweh's agent. David was a theologian par excellence.

To determine your hope, remind yourself: This is God's world and He has promised to bring a people to Himself before He shuts down the present world and brings the new heavens and the new earth. Then ask: What is your hope? Is it in God and His promises—which is true hope lived suprasensually—or is it in something that is here today and gone tomorrow (false hope)? Remember, *you* may be the one who is here today and gone tomorrow! You must ask: then what?

Hope's Motive

Next, consider the motive behind hope. Hope is goal-oriented. It has an object. What motivates a person to hope for or in something? Since people (as we described above) are self-pleasers at heart, false hope is self-directed. Taking care of oneself is the order of the day. Such is the curse of sin. Not only is the object of false hope wrong, so, too, is its motivation. "Taking care of me, as number one" is the major preoccupation of the world. People who live with this mindset are characterized as anti-God and pro-self—at least at that moment, when faced with acting on their faith and hope. "Getting something for me" is a driving force that has been true throughout the ages and will remain a predominant pattern until Jesus returns. Nothing is new under the sun!

The spouse who wants something accomplished—from a cleaner and bigger home to being appreciated—may have set his hope on its fulfillment. He may sin to get it or sin if he does not get it. He may even use or "play" God via reminding the spouse of biblical principles. God will not be mocked or used (Galatians 6:7-9). The spouse who wants and desires must first be growing, which is the object of true hope.

On the other hand, true hope has a radically different motivation. The motive behind true hope is pleasing God by becoming more like Christ. What does that mean? In answering that question, it is important to know certain biblical truths. First, God chose believers to be in Christ in eternity past, before the foundation of the world (Ephesians 1:4). Second, being in Christ means being a child of God in His family; as such, the believer grows and changes into the likeness of his brother Jesus Christ (2 Corinthians 5:9; Hebrews 2:11). That was and is God's original design. Third, God works "all things" together in order to carry out His design of glorifying Himself and growing His people. This is accomplished as the believer becomes more like Christ (Romans 8:28-29; 2 Corinthians 3:18). Fourth, the results of a Christian's changing into Christlikeness is not only for and of God's glory (Romans 8:29), but also it is toward the believer's good. In other words, it is best for you as a believer because it is best for God.

How it is best for you? Jesus Christ is the only person that God has set His full approval upon. Becoming like Him means that God will be honored and extend to the believer the expectation (true hope!) that God would count every believer as worthy of His presence (Matthew 3:17; 17:5; 25:14-30; Luke 19:19:12-27). Because of the believer's union with Christ, what is Christ's is the believer's (Colossians 3:1-3). God has placed Jesus in the most preeminent of positions and told Him "well done, good and faithful Son" (Romans 8:29; Ephesians 1:20-22; Philippians 2:9-11; Hebrews 7:25; 9:24; 12:1-3). The believer will also hear "well done" because, and only because, he is in Christ. Because of his union with Him, what is Christ's is the believer's (the *already* AND the *not yet*). Being in Christ means that you and every believer have a place of preeminence in God's eyes and nothing will dislodge him or you from that favored position—not even personal sin, wrong decisions, or what God brings into our lives (Romans 8:35-37; 1 Peter 1:3-5). These truths are not a license for sinning but an encouragement and motivation to put off ways of pleasing self and put on ways of pleasing God. In this way, the believer is preparing himself for Heaven.

Consider these two facts: living as a God-pleaser and responding to God and His providence for His glory and the good of the kingdom AND handling all of life God's way moves you and every believer to the final destination (the *not yet*): the joy of eternity with God in the likeness of His Son (John 17:1-5). But you get a taste of Heaven now. True hope is intoxicating in that way!

Looking to Heaven and being with the Triune God is true hope and that hope motivates the believer to run the race of life with joyful anticipation (Hebrews 6:13-20; 10:19-22; 12:1-3). Since eternity begins at the time of salvation through the indwelling Holy Spirit, the believer has a foretaste of Heaven now. The Triune God has brought Heaven to the believer—the *already*—with the confidence that Heaven and the believer's place in it—the *not yet*—is safe and secure. True hope is a living reality for the *now*. In Heaven, there will be no need for hope because hope will be fulfilled!

Application

1. In what ways are faith and hope similar? How is this helpful?
2. What is true hope's object and motive?
3. What is the cognitive aspect of hope?

CHAPTER 9

Qualities of True Hope: Reasons for Its Importance

A MAJOR REASON FOR TRUE hope's utmost significance is this: there will not be significant and permanent biblical change without true hope. Consider these truths.

First, pleasing God during tough times and unpleasantness will never be a motivation, a goal, or a desire for anyone without true hope. Without true hope, people easily dismiss or reject God's plan for maturing them and His method for doing so (Romans 5:1-5; James 1:2-4; 1 Peter 1:6-7).[19] One lady who had a body she did not like told me that something that hurts so badly can't be good for anything. She did not change because she had a false hope: she expected God to treat her differently and better than He had treated Jesus.

---

19   See footnote 4 for Romans 5:1-5; James 1:2-4: *Consider it pure joy my brothers whenever you face trials of many kinds, because you know that the testing of your faith develops perseverance. Perseverance must finish its work so that you may be mature and complete not lacking in anything.* 1 Peter 1:6-7: *In this you greatly rejoice; though now for a little while you may have to suffer grief in al kinds of trial. These have come so that your faith—of greater worth than gold which perishes even though refined by fire—may be proved genuine and may result in praise, glory, and honor when Jesus Christ id revealed.*

She lived for the right *now* and failed to understand her failing body in the context of God's redemptive plan of developing Christlikeness in His people. By, and because of, God's grace she was to depend on Him and use what she didn't like as her tool to bring about God's original design for all believers– to be like Christ (Genesis 1:26-27; Ephesians 1:4). She was to learn one lesson of the cross: using what is unpleasant as a tool for growth. This view of God, self, His providence, and His ways is to some an insurmountable theological mountain to climb. As a result, her false hope led to a downward spiral of hopelessness and helplessness. She focused on what she did not have—her happiness—and not on what she had, which was a relationship with Christ. Predictably, she continued to complain of pain and a body that she did not like.

Let's look in greater detail at Romans 5:1-5. Earlier in his letter to the congregation in Rome, Paul highlighted a major feature of true hope: it does not disappoint (Romans 5:5). In verses 1-4 of Romans 5, Paul listed fruits of being justified (being judged by God as righteous because God has attributed the righteous life of Christ to the believer's account). The believer has peace with God through the person and work of Jesus Christ and the believer's union with Him through and by the Holy Spirit (5:1). In addition, the believer has access to God and with God in terms of fellowship and intimacy; as a result, he rejoices in the hope of God's glory now and later to be revealed (Romans 5:2 and 1 Peter 1:6-10).

Paul continued and presented the true believer's approach to affliction (the word indicates trouble in general): he perseveres and rejoices not because of the problem and the unpleasantness but amidst it. The believer knows that Godly endurance produces hope and approval by God and hope produces Godly endurance (Romans 5:3-4). The two are linked and vital to Christian growth. Growth in Christ is hope-engendering and is always possible for the believer irrespective of the situation.

In verse 5, Paul writes that the believer is aware that true hope does not disappoint because God does not disappoint. God's way is no reason to be ashamed. True hope enables the believer to consider himself, God, others, and God's providence (*life*) from an entirely different perspective. Hope and its expectation can't fail or shame the believer because it is backed by the fact and intimate knowledge of the Triune God's trustworthiness as the covenant-making and covenant-keeping God. As testimony, witness, and proof of these facts, our God poured His love into the hearts of every believer by the Holy Spirit (5:5). The Holy Spirit is the fulfillment of God's promise to never leave and never forsake His people. But He is more: He is the down payment, the deposit, the seal, and the guarantee of future glory in Heaven that begins in this life (2 Corinthians 1:20-22; 5:5)! The hope that God gives is the believer's hope; it does not fail because the Triune God does not fail! It was Jesus' hope, as well!

Next, consider the first eight verses of James 1 in greater detail. James, the Lord's half-brother, introduces himself as slave of God and the Lord Jesus Christ (v.1). James acknowledges that the Triune God owns him! Yet James acts with authority because that authority/leadership was entrusted to him by God. In verses 2-4 (see footnote 19) which I have previously mentioned, James urges the congregation to view circumstances from God's perspective and His purpose. James speaks of trials— situations ordained by God for the purpose of spiritual growth, specifically for refining the gift of saving faith through biblical endurance. Sadly, most believers are ignorant of the fact that the gift of saving faith and its use must be refined! Faithfulness is a fruit of saving faith and exercising it. Testing, endurance, and completeness of the man of God are linked. This is heavy theology and contrasts natural man's approach to life. The unbeliever, and sadly often the believer has an ungodly focus when faced with unpleasantness. He focuses on something else other than pleasing God.

In these verses James emphasized saving faith and faithfulness that flows from it. The Holy Spirit is teaching through James that the believer's faith is not where it should be. God deserves a faith that is pure and complete. God's goal for His children, which should be the believer's as well, is a faith that is complete and pure without any defects. That is strong language and sets the stage for the verses that follow (v.5-8: *If any of you lacks wisdom, he should ask God who gives generously to all without finding fault and it will be given to him. But when he asks he must believe and not doubt because who doubts is like a wave of the sea, tossed by the wind. That man should not think he will receive anything from the Lord; he is a double-minded man unstable in all his ways*).

James knew his congregation and people in general. Shrinking away from God and His purposes is what all men do, including believers. James takes a major step toward victory, as outlined in verses 5-8. To grow one's faith in the face of God's tough providence requires wisdom—defined here as skill—in living God's way for His glory daily. It is biblical truth applied daily with the goal of growth in Christlikeness, thereby pleasing the Triune God. God gives His wisdom and gives it wholeheartedly and generously. It is there for the asking—via prayer. The person is to pray without doubting. Doubters are people of diluted and weak faith coupled with false hope. Faith, faithfulness, true hope, endurance, growth, and wisdom are linked in a golden chain of sanctification that produces the final product—a completed bracelet.

James teaches that doubters have a moral-spiritual problem. Rather than confidence and contentment in the God of circumstances and His way, the person is a waffler. He is unsettled in all his ways (James 1:8; 4:8). He has a moral problem. He lacks faith; actually, he lacks faithfulness because as a believer he has the gift of saving faith. Further, he lacks true hope because his hope is a hope-so removal from the situation rather than growth in Christlikeness. True hope strengthens faith (and vice versa!) and the person so that the person keeps his gaze on the prize: growth in Christlikeness *now,* which is part of the *already,* and perfect fellowship and intimacy eternally, which begins in the *now.* Faith and hope with its fruit enable the believer to keep a proper vertical reference, an eternal perspective and proper thinking regarding God's control—it is good and purposeful. The focus is to be on finishing the race as a God-pleasing winner. God is glorified and the believer is satisfied. In that great sense, life is always good!

Second, we learn from God's Word that true hope produces certain fruits or characteristics in the life of a believer. One such fruit is joy, which is a fruit of the Holy Spirit (Galatians 5:22-23). Returning to Romans 5:1-5, Paul writes that believers rejoice. In verse 2, the hope of God's glory is said to be the reason for believers' joy. Paul is referring to the glorious return of Jesus and His perfect judgment. Hope, then, is forward and future-looking with a *now* application. Hopeful people are joyful people because their lives are wrapped around the Triune God. Hopeless people are joyless people.

First Peter 1:6-7 gives a similar exhortation as found in James 1 (see footnote 19). One commentator translates 1 Peter 1:6-7 with the thought that the believer should be glad and rejoice in the sadness. Peter knew that sin—sinning and/or being sinned against—leads to sadness. That was not the issue. Peter was speaking of believers rightly being sad. The sadness comes from the effects of sin, sinning, and being sinned against. Only the believer can be truly glad when there is sadness all around him because he has a sure hope. Jesus taught this to the apostles the night before He was crucified (John 16:20-22). Sadness was all around, but Jesus told them the way to gladness: it is through His cross redemptively and through theirs non-redemptively (Colossians 1:24). Self must get out of the way so that Christlikeness can and does develop. A hope-so as a destiny would not produce the desire to please God in the circumstances—only the desire to get out of them.

I repeat, true hope is important for the present reality of life, for *now* living. Paul, James, and Peter emphasize this point as noted in our previous study of these passages (Romans 5:1-5; James 1:2-4; 1 Peter 1:6-7). The believer is to do what is countercultural and counterintuitive; believers rejoice in trouble. How can that be? The believer knows God's purpose for trouble. While trouble is part and parcel of living in a fallen world, the believer knows that this is God's world and He runs it His way for His glory and the believer's good. Therefore, since God works "all things" (Romans 8:28-29)—including trouble—for the good of His people, the believer looks beyond the trouble to God's presence, promises, power, purpose, provision, plan, and activity in the

Holy Spirit. When he does that, he sees the manifold goodness of God. How so? Trouble handled God's way produces and requires the Christlike qualities of endurance, approval, faithfulness, and hope (see Hebrews 12:1-3). The believer moves forward toward the finish line anticipating receiving the crown of life (1 Corinthians 9:24-27; 2 Timothy 4:7-8; Hebrews 12:1-3; James 1:12).

Third, true hope produces endurance, which is necessary for growth in the Christian life. In the opening of his first letter to the Thessalonians (1:3: *remembering your work that comes from faith, and labor that comes from love, and endurance that comes from hope in our Lord Jesus Christ, in the presence of our God and Father*), Paul reminds his friends that hope is essential for staying the course and not growing weary. He knows that hope produces endurance, which is the ability to *hang in there,* especially when one would rather not. Endurance is not "hanging on," "accepting," "living with it," "coping," "grinning and bearing it," "handling it," or "sucking it up just one more time." No, endurance is a tenacious holding fast to biblical thinking and wanting, and as a result, responding to life—God's providence whatever they may be—in a way that pleases God. (For further study, see my book *Biblical Endurance: What It Is and How It Looks in the Christian's Life*.)

Those with false hope can do no better than just try to get by anyway they can. They will function as "acceptors," "copers," "tolerators," "suck-it-uppers," and "grinners and bearers." In contrast, truly hopeful people don't grow weary or, if they do, they are able to continue, knowing that God uses even their weariness to help them grow. They may be down but never out (2 Corinthians 1:8-10; 4:8-10).[20] Hopeful people endure because they are looking forward to receiving the completion of God's original design for them—total Christlikeness, which is the prerequisite for safely and joyfully being in the Triune God's presence eternally.

Moreover, in the opening of his first letter to the Thessalonians (1:1-3), Paul combines faith and hope with endurance. In verse three, he reminds his friends that true hope is essential for endurance—which is defined as long obedience in the same direction. Endurance is staying the course and not growing weary of doing good because the prize is so great and worthy of endurance. Therefore, there is an intensity that accompanies endurance. As a result, the believer, and only the believer, continues to respond to God's providence in a way that pleases God. As a result, the person becomes more like Christ in thought, desire, and action. The believer rejoices!

---

20   2 Corinthians 1:8-10: *We do not want you to be uninformed, brother, about the hardships we suffered in the province of Asia. We were under great pressure far beyond our ability to endure, so that we despaired even of life. Indeed in our hearts we felt the sentence of death. But this happened so that we might not rely on ourselves but on God who raises the dead. He has delivered us from such a deadly peril and he will continue to deliver us. 4:8-10: We are afflicted in all sorts of ways but not crushed; perplexed but not given to despair; persecuted, but not deserted; struck down, but not destroyed; always carrying around the death of Christ in our bodies so that the life of Jesus Christ might appear in our bodies.*

Hopeful people may grow weary, but they continue, knowing that God uses even their weariness to grow them (2 Corinthians 5:9; Philippians 2:12-13). Since their overriding desire is to honor God, they hopefully endure and endure hopefully. Such was the mindset of Jesus Christ—He came to please His Father and do His will, which He accomplished by enduring the cross and despising its shame (Hebrews 12:1-2). He ran the race as a winner and to obtain the crown of glory (Hebrews 12:3). Jesus is the ultimate Endurer and believers are to imitate Him. His victory is their victory.

Fourth, another quality that is closely associated with and produced by true hope is stability or steadfastness. These terms reflect God's character. They emphasize that the believer can and should be a trusting person, because God and His promises are trustworthy, and the believer is united to the Triune God in Christ by the Holy Spirit. Further, they emphasize that the believer can, should be, and will be a hopeful truster and a trusting hoper as he imitates Christ.

The author of the book of *Hebrews* hoped to encourage his readers who were tempted to reject Christ and return to Judaism. He focused their attention on the Sufficient Christ as the author of a better covenant and who paved the way for properly enduring difficult times God's way. Therefore, the author exhorts his congregation to faithfulness in and to Christ by emphasizing Jesus' superiority to what God in the Old Testament revealed, including angels (chapter 1), Moses (chapter 3), and the Levitical priesthood and the system of sacrifice (chapters 7-10). These were excellent and glorious, but God used them to point to a greater reality and more glorious way—Jesus Christ (2 Corinthians 3:7-18).

In chapter 6, the author stressed the certainty of God's promises and God's faithful trustworthiness as an anchor for the believer and the essence of hope (verses 13-20; see footnote 10). In verse eighteen, he encouraged the readers to take hold of the hope set before them. What is the hope of which he speaks and how does one hold on to it? Among other things, it is the person and work of Jesus Christ who has entered Heaven (verses 19-20). Again, the Bible stresses knowledge and a cognitive aspect of saving faith and true hope. Since Christ is safe and secure as He awaits His return, his readers are safe and secure, but that hope is accomplished only if they hold firmly to Christ. They were to make their hope a priority because they made Christ their priority. The Holy Spirit is a down-payment on and testimony to these facts (2 Corinthians 1:20-22; 5:5; Ephesians 1:14). Therefore, there is no other anchor under the sun by which a believer can depend. Otherwise, the person is a vacillator, tossed about in the sea of God's providence (James 1:8; 4:8). In effect, they toss themselves about because their anchor is a false hope—which is no hope at all.

Hope is to be anchored in the finished work of Christ Who is in Heaven as the Victor, having completed His mission of saving a people for Himself. The author considered true hope to be essential for remaining firm and committed to Christ when faced with a decision to apostatize. People with false hope are unwise and waver; they are tossed about by the winds and waves of life—God's providence (James 1:5-8). However, they are not victims but are without a true hope because they are unbelievers or believers functioning as an unbeliever! In contrast, biblically hopeful people stay the course just as Christ stayed His course (John 12:23-28; Hebrews 12:1-3). They don't have a divided allegiance. They are wise, and they have the confidence that God answers prayers (James 1:5-8; 4:8).[21]

This message is very similar to Peter's message given in 1 Peter 1:3-5, as we have previously discussed. The safety and security of believers is firmly established and kept in Heaven by God. This heavenly activity of the Triune God was to motivate Peter's congregation to hold firmly to the reality of the object of their hope. They were to experience—taste and see—that God is good (Psalm 34:8). They were to make hope a priority. Hope is to be anchored in the Triune God and the finished work of Christ applied by the Holy Spirit. Here we

---

21   James 1:5-8: *So if any one of you lacks wisdom, let him ask God for it, since He gives everyone unreservedly and without reproaching, and it will be given to you. But let him ask in faith without doubting because a person who doubts is like a wave of the sea that is driven and tossed by the wind. That person shouldn't suppose that he will receive anything from the Lord, because a double-minded man is unstable in all his ways.* James 4:8: *Draw near to God and He will draw near to you. Wash our hands, you sinners, and purify your hearts, you double-minded persons.*

see an aspect of the *already* (salvation and its fruits via Christ in Heaven after completing His task and fulfilling John 14:1) and the *not yet* (the author's readers not in Heaven—they were still on earth).

The author considered hope to be essential when faced with the decision of rejecting Christ by returning to Judaism. Hopeless people waver, as noted by James. They are unwise, fearful, and doubting Christians. They're an oxymoron, an anomaly, that should not be. But sadly it is as part of the curse. Instead of endurance, steadfastness, and long obedience in the same direction, they vacillate in terms of their commitment to pleasing God or pleasing self (James 1:5-8; 4:8). They either attempt to get out of the race, sit on the sidelines, or change teams—they often move back under satanic control either because they are not a believer, they are people of little faith, or they do not know how to exercise their faith and hope.

Fifth, further in the book of *Hebrews*, the writer brings his readers to another characteristic produced by hope. In chapter 7, verse 19, the author is speaking about drawing near to God in the context of Christ's priesthood contrasted with the Levitical priesthood. In verses 13-20, he writes that Jesus ushered in a new and better covenant by which we draw near to God. The writer focused on intimacy and fellowship with God through Christ. The better hope of verse 19 is based on the superior High Priest, Jesus, Who is the royal, eternal, indestructible High

Priest (7:23-30); and on Christ's covenant fulfillment through His active (perfect law-keeping) and passive obedience (His perfect death) as noted in Hebrews 8:1-13.

Hopeless people draw away from God; in contradistinction, true hope draws the believer to God and away from self and biblically hopeful people draw near to Him (Ephesians 2:18; 3:12). Drawing near to God means fellowship and intimacy. The fact that the holy Triune God of the universe has saved sinners so that they may enter in and enjoy His presence is simply mind-boggling—or it should be! It is truly hope-engendering. True hope motivates a person so that the person can't get enough of the Triune God! The writer of *Hebrews* had no qualms or misgivings about presenting this theology to hurting people in serious times. Their lives depended on it (6:4-6)![22]

Drawing near to God meant staying firm in and to Christ instead of returning to Judaism. In chapters 12-13 of the book of Hebrews, the author laid out specifics for doing this. You might take the time to read those chapters as you answer the questions at the end of the section. Drawing near to God for you and me means an increasing awareness of and appreciation

---

22   Hebrews 6:4-6: *We will do this because it is impossible for renew again to repentance those who have once been enlightened who have tasted of the heavenly gift and have become sharers of the Holy Spirit, and have tasted the goodness of God's Word and the miracles of the coming age, if they fall away because they themselves crucify God's Son all over again and publicly disgrace Him. These are strong words. The writer was impressing upon his people that a return to Judaism was a declaration that they had never been a believer* (See Hebrews 10:26-31; 1 John 2:19).

for our relationship to God through Christ. It is rejoicing in the fact that Christ is our hope and has run the race for us to follow (Colossians 1:27). This relationship impacts how you think and act daily (Galatians 2:20).[23]

Sixth, another characteristic of hope is found in the First Book of John. John begins by expressing amazement at God's love and the believer's adoption. In the third chapter, verse 1, John expresses amazement that flows from his own limited comprehension of God's love. The subject of that amazement was the Fatherhood of God rightly understood.[24] John will refer to God as the Fountainhead of love in chapter 4. God demonstrated His love by sending His Son to die for undeserving sinners (4:7-9). Prior to the statement of truth, John pictured God the Lover as Father in chapter 3. John was declaring the true Fatherhood of God. John was further amazed that believers would see God as He is. John was piling up truth on top of truth in order to strengthen the hope of his people.

In verse 1, John wrote that God as Father and His adoption of sinners was incomparably amazing. In verse 2, he holds out

---

23   Galatians 2:20: *I have been crucified with Christ and I no longer live but Christ lives in me. And the life I now live in the flesh I live by faith from God's Son Who loved me and gave Himself up for me.*

24   1 John 3:1-3: *See what amazing love the Father has given to us, that we should be called the children of God—and we are! It is for this reason that the world doesn't know us, because it didn't know Him. Dear friends, we are God's children now, but it doesn't yet appear what we shall be. We know that when it does appear we shall be like Him, because we shall see Him as He is. Whoever has this hope in Him purifies himself in order to become pure like Him.*

true hope: believers will see God as He is (the promise is part of the *already* which points to the *not yet*). Christ's first coming ushered in the promise and expectation of the second coming and fellowship in eternity—the *not yet* (John 1:1-5). A part of the *not yet* that the believer has access to is viewing God as He is. The *already* is seen in verse 3: whoever has this hope is saved and will grow and change in this life.

In verse 3, John writes that having this hope (the *now* and *already*) enables the believer to live in a radically different manner: *Whoever has this hope in Him purifies himself in order to become pure like Him.* John uses the word "purify," which means setting oneself apart from sin to God's service—be holy as I am holy (Leviticus 11:44-45; Matthew 5:48; 1 Peter 1:16). The way believers do so is by growing and changing. Hopeful people are those who are growing and changing into greater Christlikeness as members of God's family. Hopeless people are not. They grow more into the likeness of Satan!

Believers live as true children of God because of their confident trust and hope in the promised reality of being in the presence of God and not being destroyed. This truth gives hope and joy for the present life. John uses the word "purification," which means setting yourself apart from sin, self, and Satan to God and His service. Believers will do that by growing and changing as part of the *already* while anticipating the *not yet*.

Application

1. The goal of life is what? See Romans 8:28-29; 2 Corinthians 5:9.

2. Hope produces or is associated with at least six qualities mentioned in this section. What are they and what is your opinion of each?

3. Hope never does what, according to Romans 5:5?

4. How do you know that God is good?

5. What evidence do you seek out to demonstrate that God does keep His promises and is worthy of your trust?

6. What specific promises of God have you hidden in your heart and how have you used them to build hope and trust?

7. What have been the results of your study of hope?

8. In what ways do you need to grow in true hope? Be specific.

CHAPTER 10

Who Needs True Hope: Results and Consequences of True and False Hope

WHO NEEDS TRUE HOPE? EVERYBODY needs true hope! Man needs a change from the issue of a misdirected and false hope to the goal of true hope. This need is more acute in some people than in others, and some people are more aware of their need than others. Who are they? The unsaved need true hope. The unsaved person realizes that he needs hope, but he sets out to find it in anything but God (Romans 1:18-20; Ephesians 2:1-3).

People are like sponges—when they are squeezed, what is inside their heart comes out in terms of hopes, thoughts, desires, and actions. God uses His providence and both hard and easy times to squeeze a person so that his heart motivation and orientation is exposed (Hebrews 3:13; 4:12). Outside pressure/hard times and good times expose a person's treasure and hope, whether the hope is false or true (Deuteronomy 8:2, 16-18; Proverbs 30:7-8; Matthew 6:19-21).[25]

Only believers have true hope, but believers can function as if their hope is a false hope.

True hope must be renewed daily (2 Corinthians 4:16-18) and that renewal comes from the study, understanding, and application of Scripture (Romans 15:4, 13). Hope is not zapped into you; true hope is God's gift through the Bible. The Holy Spirit using His Word imparts hope. He does not work apart from the Bible and He does not work against you. He works in and with you. Since the believer is a changed person, he has true hope, the resources to develop that hope, and the command to act, think, and desire in accordance with it (1 Corinthians 15:19; 1 Peter 1:13). In this sense, true hope needs to be refined and grow.

---

25   Deuteronomy 8:2, 16-18: *Remember how the Lord your God led you all the way in the desert these forty years to humble you and test you in order to know what was in your heart, whether or not you would keep his commands;" "He gave you manna to eat in the desert, something your fathers had never known, to humble you and test you so that in the end it might go well with you. You may say to yourself, "My power and strength of my hands have produced this wealth by me. But remember the Lord your God for it is he who gives the ability to produce wealth and so confirms his covenant which he swore to your forefather which as it is today.* Proverbs 30:7-9: *Two things I ask of you, O Lord; do not refuse me before I die; Keep falsehood and lies far from me; give me neither poverty nor riches; but give me only my daily bread. Otherwise, I may have too much and disown you and say, "Who is the Lord?" Or I may become poor and steal, and so dishonor the name of my God.* Matthew 6:19-21: *Don't store up treasures on earth for yourselves, where moth and rust ruin them and where thieves dig through and steal. But store up treasures in heaven for yourselves, where neither moth nor rust can ruin them, nor thieves dig through and steal. Where our treasure is there is where your heart will be too.*

Those in the heat and pressures of life (God's providence) from whatever cause need hope. God's providence may include body problems, old age, relational issues to those married and unmarried, and many others. It may be related to so-called good times, such as those who enjoy good health and even good fortune. The writer of Proverbs wrote that he did not want riches or poverty because each carried their own liabilities and the ease of denying God (Proverbs 30:97-9).

Only believers have true hope and yet they still function at various times as if they have false hope. Whenever a believer chooses to please himself, he has opted to rely on the false hope developed when he was a member of the kingdom of darkness. His hope centers on his wants and desires that often feel like demands. He may be concerned about others, but that concern may be tainted by self.

It is worth repeating that the Triune God in His Word teaches believers that true hope produces certain fruits or characteristics in the life of a believer. One such fruit is joy, which is a fruit of the Holy Spirit (Galatians 5:22-23). I return to Romans 5. In Romans 5:1-5 (see footnote 4), which we have studied in various sections, Paul writes that believers rejoice. In verse 2, he gave the reason for the believer's glory—the hope of God's glory. Paul is referring to the present reality of salvation and awaiting the glorious return of Christ and His perfect judgment. True hope, then, is forward—and future—

looking with a *now* application. Hopeful people are joyful people, and hopeless people are joyless people. Those with true hope put into practice Colossians 3:1-3.[26] Hopeful people are busy focusing on God and His promises and expecting the fulfillment of all that God has promised. But those with false hope are joyless because their focus is on themselves and their happiness, not holiness, which is God's design for all believers.

True hope is necessary for Godly living in the present reality of daily life (*now*). Believers are saved—the *already*—as they eagerly and excitedly anticipate Heaven (the *not yet*). True hope motivates the believer to keep a forward, eternal perspective. In verse 3, Paul writes that believers rejoice in trouble. How can that be? James, in James 1:2-4 (as previously noted), and Paul give God's answer: the believer knows God's purpose for trouble. While trouble is part and parcel of living in a fallen world, the believer knows that this is God's world and He runs it His way for His glory and the believer's good. Therefore, since God works "all things" (Romans 8:28-29)—including trouble—for the good of His people, the believer looks beyond the trouble to God's presence, promises, power, purpose, provision, plan, and activity in the Holy Spirit. When he does, he sees the manifold goodness of God. How

---

26 Colossians 3:1-3: *So then if you were raised together with Christ, seek the things that are above, where Christ is seated at God's right hand. Keep your mind on things that are above, not on those things that are on earth; you died and our life is hidden with Christ in God.*

so? Trouble handled God's way produces Christlike qualities of endurance, approval and hope (see Hebrews 12:1-3). The believer is becoming more like Christ, thus fulfilling the Triune God's Covenant of Redemption or Counsel of Peace established in eternity past. The believer moves toward and is moved forward toward the finish line in anticipation of receiving the crown of life (1 Corinthians 9:24-27; 2 Timothy 4:7-8; Hebrews 12:1-3; James 1:12).

Some may not agree with the Bible's definition of victory (See footnote 12). Becoming more like Christ may not seem like much of a victory for them. Rather, their focus is relief and better feelings. The Bible does not minimize misery and trouble. But it does maximize grace. In that way, believers learn more and more to trust and run the race God's way for His glory.

Moreover, true hope is a present reality for daily life and "right now" living. In Romans 5:3, Paul wrote that believers rejoice in trouble. They do so because they know God's purpose for trouble. While trouble is part and parcel of living in a fallen world, Christians know that this is God's world and that He runs it His way. Post-fall, even after salvation, the believer is continuing to become like Christ. This process, called progressive sanctification, continues until Jesus returns. Therefore, since God works "all things" (including trouble) for the good of His people, the believer looks beyond the trouble to God's presence, activity, and purpose.[27] That is where his true home and destiny is! When he does, he sees the manifold goodness of God because he knows that Christlikeness is God's original design and trouble is one of God's methods for change. It is not the trouble, per se, but the believer's use of it that is the key.

Trouble handled God's way produces the Christ-like qualities of endurance, proven character, and hope. These are the bedrock for true hope, which never disappoints (See footnote 4: Romans 5:3-5; also see footnote 2, 20). How can true hope disappoint? It can't, because it is based on God and His promises, which never disappoint. Sadly, many people (including believers) are disappointed in God because He does not perform to suit them. Rather, true hope is another of the Father's gifts to His children. He rightly expects a return on His giving. When His children are disappointed, it may be because their hope was false. In that case, every child of God must reexamine his hope. That takes us back to 1 Peter 1:13.

Often a person has the hope and expectation (even a demand) of relief or having a different body. True help, for him, requires a change in his hope. Ultimately, God wants to move him to a true hope. God hasn't made a mistake or somehow forgotten or ignored him because of his problems physical or otherwise.

---

27   Romans 8:28-29: see footnote 5. Proverbs 16:4: *The Lord works out everything for His own ends—even the wicked for a day of disaster.*

True hope helps him focus on pleasing God and honoring Him when it is hard to do so rather than finding relief.

Some Results of True and False Hope

People who have false hope are nomads. They are wanderers because false hope is dependent on the *"right now"* (Philippians 3:19). Again, their interpretative life grid is the senses—to be filled up for self and to self. They live sensually, uncontrolled by biblical truth. Esau is a prime example (Genesis 25:29-35). Paul teaches that those with false hope have their belly as their god—their feelings—and their glory is their shame—the sin of self-pleasing (Philippians 3:19-20). Such was Esau, who had little concern for the covenant and his position as firstborn. He wanted to feel *good* through filling his belly. Pleasing God was not on his radar! He put himself on the throne. At least Adam and Eve in the Garden recognized their shame and guilt, and sought to hide it with fig leaves.

Paul writes in Philippians (3:17-20) that the person who lives based on false hope glories in his sin and guilt! But the mindset that drives the mantra of *I want right now* can never guarantee or continue to guarantee what the person wants and even craves. The demands of false hope rarely remain status quo. As *"the right now"*—what a person wants and hopes for at the moment and perhaps as a patterned lifestyle—changes, his response to people and situations changes. Remember there is no truly hopeless person. Everyone has hope and seeks to have it fulfilled. The problem is the hope itself and the hope-setter.

The person whose hope is false doesn't like change or respond well to change. Because change is the essence of human life in a fallen world, false hope will never be fulfilling or feel truly satisfying. Because false hope is dependent on *me* getting or not getting and on the *now*, its object changes, and achieving it is not certain. Even if it is achieved, false hope requires constant manipulation and effort.

Getting what is hoped for that is based on false hope is a *hoped so uncertainty* that may or may not come to pass. If it does, it is almost never satisfying. This focus works against true hope. Uncertainty breeds an anticipation that leads to hopelessness and helplessness—what is often called "dashed hopes." Something that is not guaranteed and not necessarily attainable is elusive. Some descriptions that come to mind that may be old-fashioned include trying to catch a cloud in your hand, or a finding a pot of gold at end of the rainbow, an older rendition such as like the elusive "Butterfly of Love" song or Marie, the will of the wisp as she is described in the *Sound of Music*. The excitement may come in trying to get a hold of it, but that, too, wearies a person. Futility, uncertainty and even bondage to either what is hoped for or the pursuit of attaining it are the consequences of placing your hope in a false object—something other than Jesus Christ and His promises.

Consider another example. There is the hope that is based on a person changing: spouse, child, boss, or friend. It may be centered on the desire for a different body, diseased or not. The person eagerly anticipates and expects change. He is busy wanting others to change and judging them and God. The person is so busy with others that he does not focus on what he was saved to do: please God by becoming more like Christ. The person and the situation may not change, and they will probably tell you that their hopes were dashed.

True hope, on the other hand, results in an increased capacity and desire to grow and change in Christlikeness. People with true hope grow in their ability to think, desire, and act like Jesus. They simply can't get enough of Jesus and the Triune God. They are interested in glorifying God by growing and changing, developing more of the Son's likeness. This is what the believer was saved for: to prepare for life in Heaven. Believers know that it is best for them as well as for the will of the Triune God. When hard times come, they are not devastated. They are not hopeless. In response, they will use hard times as God's instrument for them to mature in their faith and hope. In this way, life is simplified and the choices before them are limited by their motivation to please God as they become and enjoy becoming more like Christ. That is true hope—that is relief! They begin to more and more rely on the promises of God that He will never leave or forsake them and that He provides wisdom and strength. Basically, God provides Himself! Job discovered this truth (Job 38-42) and David proclaims it (Psalm 34:8).

How will true hope relied upon and exercised look in a believer's life? He must be secure in his God: He is a present, powerful, promise-making and –keeping God, Who has blessed His people. Faced with hard times, the person will ask, what is my hope? His answer clears the air and helps him honestly ask other questions such as: Are the issues getting out of the situation instead of growing in it; getting better and relief or changing and growing in Christlikeness; or on the other person changing rather than on self. In those simple snippets of life scenarios, the person's heart is exposed for his good. He puts off his false hope and puts on true hope.

Application

1. Compare and contrast true and false hope. What do you learn?

2. Hope is related to and evidenced by the orientation and activity in man's heart. Jesus' words in Matthew 6:19-21 and 24-34 focus on man's heart activity. How do they relate to true and false hope?

3. True hope enables believers to interpret the now by the not yet. In that way, the believer is to be of earthly good. Reread Colossians 3:1-3 and 1 John 3:1-3: how do these passages explain this truth?

CHAPTER 11

How to Give Hope

LET'S REVIEW WHERE WE HAVE come thus far. Hope has the following features: it is something everybody has. Hope, both true and false hope, is common, universal, and necessary for life; it motivates, it involves knowledge and trust, and it requires a choice. It is part of God's creational design of man. Everyone has hope, and yet everyone doesn't have *true hope,* as a result of the fall and God's judgment. True hope is a gift, and hoping—the expression and exercise of hope—is commanded.

When true and false hope were contrasted, we discovered that true hope has its object, the Triune God, and its motivation is the desire to please God by becoming more like Christ. It results in a lifestyle characterized by pleasing God daily in thought, desire, and action. False hope is something every person has because Adam sinned. This hope is misdirected and false, focusing on self as the getter. The good news is that false hope can be changed, and true hope is available to all who are in Christ.

The next question is vital: how do I get and give true hope? We know the preliminary answer to that question: I can't, and you can't. But God can and does! Hope is given, and in abundance, by God through the Holy Spirit, Who uses His Word (the Bible) to give it to believers (Romans 15:4, 13). Salvation is the key. If one is an unbeliever, he can be brought to the point where he becomes aware of the falseness of his hope and the futility that results from its pursuit. The unbeliever doesn't have the indwelling Holy Spirit. He has ears but doesn't hear and eyes but doesn't see. He can only interpret the information he receives sensually—without the aid of biblical truth. He has hope, but it is no hope at all.

You can speak to the unbeliever about Jesus and you can follow Christ's example by modeling true hope. God may be pleased to use you to come alongside others—both unbelievers and believers—to bring God's truth to the one who is drowning in a sea of bad feelings and hopelessness. Consider a rewording of the question. Ask the believer how he can be an effective servant of God and give hope to those who are fighting God, when so often they deny that they are.

The unbeliever is unable to discern and understand life from God's perspective. He has ears but doesn't hear, and eyes but doesn't see what is spiritually discerned (Matthew 13:13; 1 Corinthians 2:14).[28] On the other hand, the believer, who is a new creature in Christ indwelt by the Holy Spirit, can understand life

---

28   Matthew 13:13: *This is the reason I speak to them in parables, because though they see, they don't see and though they hear, they don't hear; nor do they understand. 1 Corinthians 2:14: But a natural person doesn't welcome the teachings of God's Spirit; they are foolishness to him and he isn't able to know about them because they must be investigated spiritually.*

from God's perspective (2 Corinthians 5:17: see footnote 11). In helping people develop true hope, both believer and unbeliever, it is important to speak with them, and even warn them, about the toughness of life apart from Christ (Proverbs 13:15; Psalm 32:10).[29]

As said previously, an unbeliever has false and misdirected hope. He can be brought to the point where he becomes aware of the futility of his hope and the bondage that results from its pursuit. His *hope-so* will always be just that, unless he is saved. Salvation is the key. Therefore, the most hope-producing activity one can do for the unbeliever is to present the gospel message that Christ lived, died, and rose from the dead for undeserving sinners, and He beckons them to come to Him for rest (Matthew 11:28-30; 1 Corinthians 15:1-4).[30] The gospel message, which includes salvation and life after salvation in Christ by the Holy Spirit, must be presented in the most relevant manner given the person, the presenter's relation with him, the person's willingness to hear, and his spiritual maturity (see Acts 14, 16, 17 for examples of audience adaptation).

True hope is given in abundance to the believer as he uses the Bible to solve problems and respond to life situations God's

---

29   Proverbs 13:15b: *Good understanding wins favor but the way of the transgressor is hard.* Psalm 32:10: *Many are the woes of the wicked but the Lord's unfailing love surrounds the man who trusts Him.*

30   Matthew 11:28-30: *Come to Me, all who labor and are heavily burdened, and I will refresh you. Put My yoke on you and learn from Me; I am meek and humble in heart; and you will discover refreshment for your souls. My yoke is easy to wear and My burden is light.*

way (Romans 15:4, 13: see footnote 9, 12). When the believer has seemingly "lost" his way and views things as hopeless, he is functioning as an unbeliever. He has determined that his resources for handling his failed expectations are depleted. He is attempting to understand God through the circumstances rather than his circumstances through the Scripture and the indwelling Holy Spirit. His problems appear to be much larger than himself and the God of those circumstances. He is functioning as if the Creator God is small and inadequate for his situation. He may also think of God as just another person to give him what he thinks he needs. Only a proper view of the God of true hope will enable the Christian to respond to circumstances God's way.

To help a believer develop true hope, it is necessary to start where the person is. He may not acknowledge that he is responsible for his hopelessness. He may not be aware or understand 1 Peter 1:13. It may be a matter of ignorance, arrogance, or both. Help him differentiate true and false hope in the context of his situation. There are at least two ways to help a person differentiate true and false hope. First, if the hope-expectation is forbidden by God, it is a false hope. He must repent. You should ask him why having it is so important and why having it at God's expense doesn't seem to matter. Second, if the person sins to get it or sins if he does not get it, it is a false hope. To unbelievers, self-pleasing and self-fulfillment is more important than pleasing God. The person may be functioning as an idolater.

Most everyone has established several false hopes. But not everyone responds to them in the same manner and for the same reasons in their pursuit or its lack of fulfillment. It is important to determine a person's spiritual maturity and willingness to learn and to give the biblical truth that best fits the person and his situation. Remember that hope is essential for Godly living. You must reach the person through their thinking and wanting. To accomplish that, have the person define the problem, his solution and reasons for his choice, and the results (hope) he envisions. Often, the person has defined the problem and solution his way at God's expense. He is hopeless because he is depending on someone or something other than God and His solution.

Help the person acknowledge that his troubles are only the context in which he acts upon his hope. It is important to tailor God's manifold truth to meet the person in the context of his situation. True hope is built on the firm foundation of hearing and obeying God's word (Matthew 7:24-27). These verses teach that everyone is a house builder and hearer of God's word; however, only the believer builds his house on the firm foundation of hearing and obeying Christ's teaching.

In any one-on-one ministry, follow the axiom of listen to learn to love, to lead into biblical truth and freedom.

Therefore, in the office, when a patient expresses his idea of hope in terms of pain relief and removal of bodily problems, I ask questions challenging the person's hopes, expectations, fears and wants. You must get behind the scenes, so to speak, and find out what is behind his hope and expectation. Often the person and his hope are on the throne of the person's heart and this hope is manifested as a demand. Ask how he perceives himself in the context of the unpleasantness. You want to know how his situation has morphed into one of hopelessness. What is the hope that he has not achieved, and what makes it so important? Most of the time, people with aches and pains are concerned about the possibility of the potential of no relief and of loss of function. In other words, the person's hope is to function as he always did, but he now perceives that he can't. In response, the person has labeled himself hopeless. However, these people aren't hopeless: they simply have misdirected and false hope.

Explore a person's thinking and wanting. You do that by bringing God into the picture. Often, I ask: Has God made a mistake by allowing you to be in the position you find yourself? That is a bottom-line question: the answer gives the direction to take. If he believes that God makes mistakes and his condition is a prime example, you must challenge that line of reasoning. His problem is with God. No change toward moving him to true hope can occur if his view of God is sinful.

Challenge a person's thinking by helping him see the unattainability of his hope. Have him define his hope and then ask: "What is the reality of living in a fallen world in your condition without pain and discomfort?" His reality may be a sin-cursed body, God's unpleasant providence, and medical care that may or may not reverse the problem. We must determine if the person with "dashed hopes"—not getting what he wants and hopes for—has faced the fact that he may not get what he hopes and wants. I continue that line of thinking by asking him to tell me how he was pursuing his hope and the results of that pursuit. I also ask him what happens when he doesn't get what he hopes for or wants. I want him to be aware that desires may be good or bad. I repeat: a bad desire is one directly forbidden by God. They are always wrong to pursue. A good desire may be sinful when its importance is elevated to a status equal to or above pleasing God. How can you tell? The status of any desire can be determined by how one proceeds to fulfill it and how he responds when he doesn't get it.

The desire to be pain-free or to have good health is not necessarily wrong if it fits into an overall program of good stewardship of the body. Good stewardship is the privilege and responsibility of all believers, but being disease- or pain-free is not. If one's hope is a pain-free body or relief no matter what, and the person desperately pursues any number of approaches to achieve this goal, then pleasing God is not his motive. People will indulge any number of unproven remedies and activities in hopes of ensuring good health. More often than not, his merry-go-round only causes more problems.

On the other hand, people may be interested in good health as part of a program of good stewardship. Be sure to ask: "What happens if you don't get your hope or desire?" Often, I hear the cycle characterized by an intensification of his pursuit, a more focused thinking and activity on getting what he wants, and more pain—entirely different than what he hoped. When he doesn't get what he wants, ask him what he is thinking and watch how he responds. Many times, the person responds in resentment, anger, bitterness, fearfulness, and worry. He may be labeled as depressed. If you have been following closely, in a real sense he has "depressed" himself! Often, these responses are brushed off as givens, "normal," "understandable," and/or frustration due to his problems. God's providential control is never considered. The person's response to the problem is not considered, either, and he is usually medicated.

The person is not familiar with or denies the fact that his response worsens him in his situation, which leads to and intensifies the hopelessness cycle. By that I mean, when people don't get what they want and respond in a less than God-pleasing manner, the desire becomes a want which becomes a demand. When these are not met, the person sees his situation as hopeless and himself as helpless. The cycle continues, and as a result, his responses of anger, bitterness, and resentment only intensify. As a result, there is more futility, bondage, mad so-called dashed hopes. The person can actually think himself "sick." A person's attitude affects a person's well-being (Proverbs 12:25; 14:30; 15:13, 30; 16:24; 17:22).

Help the person see where his pursuit of his hope has gotten him. If you succeed, he will view his pursuits differently. He will recognize the futility and counterproductive nature of his efforts. Seeking his "hope" has resulted in hopelessness. Awareness of both the false hope and the pursuit of it are potent motivators in helping a person change from false hope to true hope. In addition, using biblical terminology whenever possible redefines the person's true state. By that I mean use words that God uses in His Word to describe a person's thinking, wanting, and responding. Frustration is anger, bitterness is discontent, and feeling sorry for self is self-pity. Using God's definition of the problem and His description of the person's response allows an easier transition to bring God's solution to light. Doing it this way will help move a person from human reasoning to God's wisdom and freedom.

Lastly, you must help people put something in the place of their false hope. You do that by maximizing God's solution in the heat of the problem. Having shown them the end result of false hope, in contrast, show them the beauty of true hope. That beauty is, in part, found in its simplicity. How so? Pleasing God is always attainable. One need never wonder whether circumstances or people will change. They don't need to change. The person is sufficient in Christ and therefore *all things* are to be used for God's glory and the believer's good. That means using what he doesn't like to grow and change, developing more the character of Christ. Becoming more like Christ is always attainable. That is true victory and the basis for true hope.

The person with false hope will need help in accomplishing this holy and blessed responsibility, privilege, and duty. You want to help him change his view of becoming more like Christ. It is a blessing and privilege because the Triune God is honored and magnified. Help him redefine his thinking and wanting in terms of his relationship with Christ. As he thinks and desires as Jesus did (John 4:31-34), his hope will change and he will endure, rejoice, grow and change. He will draw closer to God and hold fast to the only One who can bring him home to Heaven. That is true hope! As a result, he will rejoice in his present reality (2 Corinthians 12:7-10).

Application

1. What does the axiom: listen, to learn, to love, to lead into what?
2. What challenges are important when addressing true and false hope?
3. How do you replace false hope with true hope? Each are based on promises: what are they?

CHAPTER 12

Specific Truths for Daily Living: Developing and Maintaining True Hope

CONSIDER SPECIFIC KEY CONCEPTS AND passages useful for helping a person get victory as you help him develop and rely on true hope.

One: Pleasing God in unpleasantness is accomplished by using hard times to grow and change (see footnote 12 for definition of victory). This is a John 4:31-34 and 2 Corinthians 5:9-15 approach to life (see footnotes 3 and 14). It served Jesus well, and believers are to imitate Christ. A self-centered approach to life is contrary to pleasing God and results from and in false hope. False hope compels a person to follow his own solution of seeking one's own comfort, relief, or well-being. A life based on false hopes will only lead to further futility and bondage (Proverbs 5:21-22; 13:15b; 26:11; Psalm 32:10).

Importance is a key feature of hope—true or false. Help the person define what he is hoping for and his ways for getting it. It is a must to help the person unravel the importance to him of having his hope fulfilled. Pursuing the person's definition of his hope (the what) is one aspect of helping him develop true hope. Another is to help him determine the why of its pursuit. Another key is the how he is pursuing it.

Two: Hope and faith are relational. True hope results in a life motivated by the goal of pleasing God which is God's design for every believer. Jesus, as the Messiah, had true hope that was anchored in His relationship with the Father: He and the Father were one (John 10:30). Therefore, He lived to please His Father and accomplish the work of the Triune God. In John 4:31-34, John teaches that pleasing the Father was Jesus' nourishment and strength, which satisfied His whole person. In those verses, Jesus contrasted the *sensual* pleasure from eating food with the *suprasensual* pleasure of pleasing His Father. The disciples went seeking after food and, upon returning, asked Jesus if He had eaten. He told them He had food to eat. The disciples assumed that this was physical food intended to fill and satisfy the body (the right *now*). Jesus advocated good stewardship and taking care of the body. Jesus was not referring to the body and its care only. He made it clear that His "food" was not simply physical. He looked beyond the physical and the sensual. He viewed His situation suprasensually based on God's Word and plan. He viewed the sensual input via His relationship with the Triune God, His purpose, His focus, and the completion of His mission. Nourishment of His whole person (body and soul) was gained by pleasing the Father. True hope enabled Jesus to focus, not on the hardships, but on the goal of being God's kind of Son Who always pleased His Father. He viewed the cross as God's instrument to accomplish redemption. Pleasing the Father motivated Him all the way to the cross and beyond.

Three: Paul and Peter, in particular, wrote that they imitate Christ (1 Corinthians 11:1; 2 Corinthians 10:1; 1 Peter 2:21). In 2 Corinthians 5:9, 14-15, Paul builds on Jesus' teaching, especially in the gospel of John, which presents pleasing God as the aim or ambition of every believer in the seen and unseen worlds. He further defines this aim in verses 14-15 when he wrote that he no longer lived for self (which is the focus and motivation of false hope), but that he lived as a God-pleaser (which is the focus of true hope).

Four: The person who has false hope may not know that victory and the key to that victory exists.[31] He may not even know that he is at war. He must be enlightened! Since every person lives out of his hope with fears, expectations, desires, and wants, he has an agenda and strategy for how best to attain his hopes and avoid his fears.

In an effort to help a believer distinguish between true and false hope, the person must be guided to acknowledge his hopes and his plans for gaining that hope. Some hopeless substitutes include "getting by," "tolerating," "coping," "getting out of the situation," and "avoiding stress." Other potential

---

31   See footnote 12 for a description of victory.

false hopes and goals include good health, relief, cure, a "better quality of life," and a return to functioning "like I used to."

Five: there is a higher level of hope than simply "getting by" that a person may have. The believer, and even the unbeliever, can make taking responsibility his hope. Being responsible is something any person can do even if he hurts or faces trouble. Being responsible is contrary to the culture's view that people are victims and thus exempt from being responsible. However, when a person is helped to function based on this hope, his life will be simplified. His desire may not be to please God, which, as we have said, is the focus of true hope. Without true hope, the person will likely become weary of being responsible. However, if he has moved from simply "getting by" to being responsible no matter his situation, he is moving in the direction of a clearer view of the God of hope. He will gain significant wisdom from his change, but we don't want him to stop there!

The goal is to move the believer from his life of "dashed hopes" to a life characterized by hopefulness. True hope is always attainable for the believer because it results from a changed heart with the implanted desire to please the Father which leads to responding to hard times in a God-honoring manner. Unfortunately, too many Christians fail to realize that living as a God-pleaser every moment of one's life is the ultimate human experience while on earth (Paul did in Philippians 3:7-11).[32] True

---

32   Philippians 3:7-11: *But whatever was gain to me I have counted loss for Christ's sake. Indeed, to put even more accurately, I count everything as loss*

hope results from one's relationship with Christ and impacts a person's thinking, motivation, and actions.

Six: Another aspect of giving true hope is to move a person toward an understanding and appreciation of God's definition of victory (see footnote 12). Since the individual has defined the problem and victory his way, he is "hopeless." His hope is false and misdirected because he is depending on solutions and results that may be different than God's. In essence, he is depending on his own resources. He may rightfully understand that he has reached the end of his resources. His hope has crumbled. However, God has him right where He wants him. That is true hope! Help him view his position from that perspective.

Seven: True hope only comes as the problem and solution according to God's Word. Only then is God's solution apparent to the person. The application of biblical wisdom will enable the believer to continue to view himself, God, and His providence according to biblical truth. That is true hope in action! For example, a husband or wife who is experiencing unpleasantness at home sees no way out except divorce, unless the spouse changes. They may even be correct in thinking that the spouse should change. Yet their hope is based on their wants

---

compared to the priceless privilege of knowing Christ Jesus my Lord for Whose sake I have suffered total loss and count what I have lost garbage in order that I may gain Christ, and be found in Him, not having a righteousness of my own that stems for the law but instead that which comes through faith in Christ the righteousness from God based upon faith.

and centers on change in the other person. They are "hopeless" because their false hopes aren't being fulfilled. The downward spiral of hopelessness and helplessness increases speed until they are not only down but out. The struggle is not with the spouse but with God, Who gifted them with their spouse. Each person faces the reality of being God's kind of husband or wife even if the other person doesn't change.

Functionally, the one spouse is attempting to thwart God's command of being a God-honoring husband or wife (See Job's response in Job 42:2-6). As a believer, each spouse can grow as a Godly spouse. The husband was never called to be his wife's Holy Spirit or her "changer." Godly change comes as his hope changes, which is an indication of an internal change! The way to help him is to have him change his hope—not his wife or his God! Life will be simplified when change is increasing in Godliness. He will begin to use what he doesn't like to become more like Christ. In this case, victory is being God's kind of husband, no matter the circumstances (Ephesians 5:25-32: the husband as a lover of his wife and 1 Peter 3:7: the husband as the learner of his wife).

In no way would we want to minimize the perceived sin of the spouse. That is not the issue. It may be an issue, depending on any number of things. But for the purpose of this book, I chose to focus on the husband and his false hope and its implications. These are general principles applicable to every believer in any situation.

Eight: Another important activity in giving true hope is using biblical terminology whenever possible as mentioned in the previous section. This helps the person redefine his true state. By that I mean we should use the Bible's terms when describing a person's thinking, wanting, and responding. For instance, many people describe their response to their situation as "frustration." These, like most, people haven't drawn the connection between outside pressure and their response to it. Actually, the biblical description of their response is anger. They blame "stress," as if what is inside and outside of them determines their response. They ascribe power to outward pressure, which causes them to think and act in a certain way.

Similarly, "bitterness" is, in fact, discontentment, "feeling sorry for oneself," or brooding, which is self-pity. Using God's definition of the problem and His description of the person's response allows an easier transition for bringing God's solution into the picture. Challenging the person's perspective in this way may move him from his use of human reasoning to embracing God's wisdom. This brings true hope!

Here are some examples of recasting a person's description of his response by using biblical terms and thinking. In the area of smoking, ask a person the reasons he smokes and add such questions as: "What does smoking do for you?" or "What do you like about it?" Another common situation is in the realm of personal relationships. When a husband says that he gets irritated at his wife, rephrase his answer to something like this: "What is it about what your wife does that makes you so angry?" "Do you have any personal responsibility in this area?" I know and God knows that his wife did not make him angry. He became angry and perhaps he is an angry person. If his hope is focused on her and her "need" to change, he is ignoring his own sinfulness.

Physicians hear patients report that "pain depresses me so much that I can't function like I want to and/or used to." Ask the person what it is about pain that depresses him, and ask him to define "can't." You get the picture. Restating the person's statements in biblical terms is intended to compel him to think more clearly about his view of cause and effect.

In addition, someone may say: "Stress makes me hurt and I feel bad, and when I feel bad I am not easy to live with." The person's hope may be to eliminate *stress*. He also may be looking for an excuse because God has not seen fit to give him what he thinks he needs and deserves. In order to help people develop true hope, they must define *stress* and tell you how *stress* is bad. *Stress* may refer to something outside of them. Some call this *life,* but in fact they are referring to God's providential control. Some refer to *stress* as what is inside a person. The person assumes that what is outside of him determines what is inside him. In fact, it is the person who responds to God and His control. The person's feelings are linked to his wanting, thinking, and hoping. The person's response is dependent on his relationship with the Triune God. A right view of God and self gives a right view of circumstances and people and results in a God-honoring response. This springs from and breeds true hope!

Removing *stress*—that which is outside—if it were possible— is not God's goal or to be the believer's goal. God runs His world His way for His glory and the good of the believer. Using the unpleasantness to become more like Christ is the proper goal and is what the believer was saved to do (Romans 8:28-29; 2 Corinthians 12:7-10).

James mentions fights and quarrels (James 4:1-3).[33] These occur because of *I wants* in the context of relationships. False hope surfaces and demands more energy and attention of the other person—for me and to me. Self-pleasing morphs into the demand of *I must have*. The person with this sinful and false hope acts as if change refers only to the other person and to God.

Moreover, chasing the false hope of the fulfillment of *I wants* and *I must have* is based on the false belief that life is for me, by me, and to me. The person's heart is exposed. Only biblical truth, rightly known and properly applied, brings light and truth to replace darkness and falsehood. In this instance, it would be

---

33   James 4:1-3: *Where do wars and where do fights come from? Isn't it from our pleasures that are warring in our bodily members? You desire something and don't have it. You murder and envy and still don't obtain it. You fight and you war. You don't have it because you don't ask! You don't receive when you ask, since you ask wrongly—to waste it on your pleasures.*

appropriate to have the person write out his view of *stress*, its source, how it is bad, his response to it, and where the Triune God fits into the picture. Help him restate his answers using biblical language.

The Bible gives clarity to what people call *stress*: being sinned against, tough times, and trouble, to mention just a few. The Bible also describes a person's sinful response in and to trouble and being sinned against as returning evil for evil, anger, bitterness, clamor, resentment and malice (Romans 12:17-21; Ephesians 4:31). When a person's description of his response to his situation is couched in biblical terms, God's solutions can be presented, which gives true hope.

Too often people identify themselves as victims, and therefore consider themselves as powerless over that which is outside of them. At other times, they seemingly take matters into their own hands. Jesus Christ, indwelt by the Holy Spirit, is considered a victim and loser by some. He is in reality the Victor, and He never took matters into His own hands. He relied on His relationship with the Triune God. Therefore, following Jesus and imitating Him is to be the focus of the believer. Jesus showed the world how to turn tragedy into triumph and to gain victory out of seeming defeat. His is one lesson of the cross: Jesus' victory is one lesson of the cross.

In contrast to Christ's response to trouble, the person with false hope responds poorly—and even sinfully—to the problem.

The problem is not the trouble; it is the person's response to what is outside of him that is the problem. His response is basically an inner-man/heart problem. The response, in part, hinges on his hope: "I hope for comfort, security, my way, ease of life, approval, and no stress." An unfulfilled hope is not the same thing as losing hope. A person's sinful response to unfulfilled hope may reflect the falseness of that hope. Calling a person to respond to trouble God's way gives hope because God doesn't give commands His people are unable to keep (1 Corinthians 10:13; 1 Peter 1:13).

Nine: There are requirements for developing true hope. The person must acknowledge the futility, bondage, and counter-productivity of his pursuit of solving problems his way (Proverbs 13:15b, Psalm 32:10: see footnote 29). Asking questions that move from the *inside-out* will challenge his hopes, expectations, fears, and wants. Find out what these are and have him clarify his definition of victory.

In the area of the physical, someone may express his idea of hope in terms of pain relief and/or removal of the bodily problem. You must get behind the scenes, so to speak, and find out what is driving his hope. You may do that by asking him how it is bad or unpleasant that his hope hasn't been fulfilled. Most of the time, people with physical problems are concerned about potential loss of function. If their hope is to function as they have previously, they may think of themselves as hopeless and eventually they develop a mindset of learned helplessness. However, these people aren't hopeless or helpless: they have misdirected and false hope, with no prospect of its fulfillment. They will deveople a learned and patterned hopelessness, which becomes their guiding light. Rather than considering the results as a gift from God, they consider God and His ways as a burden.

You may approach a person and his false hope several ways. One way is to bring God into the picture. God is already in the picture (it is His world: Psalm 24:1-2; 115:4; 135:6), but the person is functioning as if He isn't![34] Help him recognize the reality that God is there. Ask him questions such as: "Has God made a mistake by allowing you (actually God ordains it, but using *allowing* it is softer) to be in the position you are in?" That is a bottom-line question. One's answer to it reveals in which direction you need to pursue. If he believes that God makes mistakes and his condition is a prime example, you must challenge that line of reasoning. His problem is with God. He will not develop true hope as long as he views God in that light. If he believes that God hasn't made a mistake, then he may be ready to hear one of God's solutions to his problem.

Ten: Another way to help a believer to develop true hope is to challenge his thinking by helping him see the non-attainability

---

34   Psalm 24:1-2: *The earth is the Lord's, and everything in it, the world, and all who live in it; for he founded it upon the seas and established it upon the waters.* Psalm 115:3: *Our God is in heaven; he does whatever pleases him.* Psalm 135:6: *The Lord does whatever pleases him, in the heavens and on the earth, in the seas and all their depths.*

of his hope. "What is the reality of living in a fallen world with a sin-cursed body?" The reality is usually some type of physical problem and pain. Or "what is the reality of living in a fallen world with a spouse who does things you don't like?" The reality is more of the same, unless one's hope is in pleasing God, using hard times to do so.

Often it is wise to continue to probe his view of the attainability of his hope by asking him to tell you how he has pursued his hope and what the results have been. Helping the person see the results of the pursuit of his false hope will lead him to see both its futility and counter-productivity. Hopelessness results as he seeks his hope. Awareness of both the false hope and the pursuit of it are potent motivators for a person to change.

Eleven: In this area of reevaluating one's hope, it is often helpful to help a person understand that desires may be good or bad. To reiterate, a bad desire is one directly forbidden by God. These desires are always wrong to pursue, as is the hope that focuses on fulfilling them. A good desire may be bad when its importance is elevated to a status equal to or above pleasing God. One can tell the status of any desire by how one proceeds to gain it and how one responds when he doesn't get it. Desires to be pain-free, to have good health, or to have a spouse act a certain way are not necessarily wrong. However, people may be interested in obtaining a good desire for the wrong reason.

If the desire to be pain-free serves oneself at the exclusion of others, the desire is wrong and self-focused, no matter the spin he places on having it. If the desire to be pain-free or have good health fits into an overall program of good stewardship of the body, then stewardship, not freedom from pain, should be the motivation for taking care of the body.

Twelve: Good stewardship is the privilege and responsibility of all believers, but being disease- or pain-free is not. If one's hope is a pain-free body or one that isn't "too" old, and he desperately pursues any number of approaches to get it, then good stewardship is not his motive. Sadly, people use a variety of ways in order to ensure good health or to get spousal conformity according to their own standard.

In order to further clarify the status of the desire in one's heart, one can ask: "What happens if you don't get your hope and desire?" Often the answer will be an intensification of his pursuit and a more focused determination to get what he wants. When he doesn't get what he wants, ask him what he is thinking and wanting, and see how he responds. Many times the person responds with anger, bitterness, and frustration. When this happens, the hopelessness cycle moves into high gear. When people don't get what they want and respond in a non-God-honoring manner, the hope and desire have become a want elevated to a demand. When demands are not met, the person sees his situation as hopeless, and the cycle continues.

Futility and bondage are the results. This is a description of a Proverbs 13:15 and Psalm 32:10 approach to life, which contrasts that of a John 4:31-34 and 2 Corinthians 5:9-15 approach to life.

Thirteen: It is also important to help the person replace his false hope. In order to do that, one should maximize God's solution in the midst of the problem. True hope enables the person to acknowledge that his trouble is God's instrument for him to use in order to develop and further true hope.

Once the person has acknowledged the end result of false hope, he must be shown the beauty of true hope. That beauty is, in part, found in its simplicity. This is so because pleasing God is always attainable. Therefore, one need never put his hope in changing people or circumstances. God may or may not change people or circumstances, but others don't need to change for a believer to live a joyful, satisfied, and contented life. The person with true hope is sufficient in Christ and therefore uses *all things* for God's glory and his good (Romans 8:28-29). That means using what he doesn't like to grow and change, developing more of the character of Christ. This is victory, which takes grace. Becoming more like Christ is always attainable.

Helping a person to redefine his thinking and wanting in terms of his relationship with Christ puts him on the road to developing true hope. As he imitates Christ in terms of thoughts, desires, and actions (John 4:31-34), his hope will continue to change, and he will endure, rejoice, and grow as seeks true change. Changing one's hope and beliefs are fundamental to living as a victor in Christ. As a result and as part of the change process, the believer will draw closer to God and hold fast to the only One who can bring him home to Heaven. That is true hope!

Application

Of the thirteen truths named in this section, pick five that you will use regularly. Record how and when you used them, as well as what the results were.

Comparison and Contrast of True and False Hope

	False Hope	True Hope
1. Choice	Yes, yet never commanded;	Yes; it is commanded
2. Cognition	My thoughts; Culture's thoughts	John 4:31-34, 2 Corinthians 5:9, 14-15, Jesus' approach to life
3. Conviction	My way—self	Pleasing God
4. Commitment	Trust self	Trust God and His promises
5. Expectation	Happiness—mine	Holiness—to be like Christ
6. Focus/Object	The "right now": present, personal, visible, external, created temporal	Daily living with eternal focus Colossians 3:1-3; 1 John 3:1-3
7. Motive	Pleasing me	Becoming more like Christ
8. Consequence	Futility, bondage, Uncertainty	Joy, contentment, Satisfaction

Assignments to Help Evaluate Your Hope Status

1. What is your hope for today and in the days to come?

a. List the things about which you are most hopeful and why.

b. List the things that you are least hopeful about and why.

2. How do these things give you hope?

3. What certainty do you have that any of them will occur?

4. What is that certainty based upon?

5. What is your plan for attaining your hope?

6. How have you responded when your hopes are not met?

7. How does your hope compare with 1 Peter 1:13?

a. In that verse, Peter teaches that hope is a what?

b. Therefore, lack of true hope is whose responsibility?

c. What does hope rest on?

d. How did Peter expect hope to influence his people?

8. How does your hope compare with 1 Corinthians 15:19-20?

a. What is hope good for?

b. In these verses, what is the basis for the believer's hope?

c. What results did Paul expect? See 1 Corinthians 15:54-58.

9. What hope did John speak of in 1 John 3:1-3?

a. What was the basis for that hope?

b. What was the result of that hope?

c. How is the believer to live out that hope daily?

Also by Dr. Jim Halla and Ambassador International

Being Christian in Your Medical Practice

Depression Through a Biblical Lens: A Whole-Person Approach

Endurance: What It Is and How It Looks in a Believer's Life

How to Be a God-Pleasing Patient: A Biblical Approach to Receiving Medical Care

Joy in Grief: God's Answer for Hard Times

Pain: The Plight of Fallen Man

The Book of Job: God's Faithfulness in Troubled Times

For more information about
Dr. Jim Halla
&
Out of the Maze
please visit:

www.jimhalla.com
www.facebook.com/jimhalla
jimhalla@yahoo.com

For more information about
AMBASSADOR INTERNATIONAL
please visit:

www.ambassador-international.com
@AmbassadorIntl
www.facebook.com/AmbassadorIntl

www.ingramcontent.com/pod-product-compliance
Lightning Source LLC
Chambersburg PA
CBHW060357090426
42734CB00011B/2160